COGNITIVE DEVELOPMENT
IN YOUNG CHILDREN

Basic Concepts in Educational Psychology Series
Larry R. Goulet, University of Illinois, Series Editor

COGNITIVE DEVELOPMENT IN YOUNG CHILDREN

NANCY EWALD JACKSON
University of Washington

HALBERT B. ROBINSON
University of Washington

PHILIP S. DALE
University of Washington

BROOKS/COLE PUBLISHING COMPANY
MONTEREY, CALIFORNIA

A Division of Wadsworth Publishing Company, Inc.

Printed in the United States of America

10 9 8 7 6 5 4 3 2 1

Library of Congress Cataloging in Publication Data

Jackson, Nancy Ewald.
 Cognitive development in young children.

 (Basic concepts in educational psychology)
 Based on a report with the same title prepared by the authors for the Na-
tional Institute of Education and published in 1976.
 Bibliography: p. 71
 Includes index.
 1. Cognition in children. I. Robinson, Halbert B., joint author. II.
Dale, Philip S., joint author. III. Title.
BF723.C5J29   370.15'2   77-1725
ISBN 0-8185-0225-8

Production Editor: *John Bergez*
Interior and Cover Design: *Linda Marcetti*
Illustrations: *Katherine Minerva*

SERIES FOREWORD

The present time is an exciting period in the history of education. We are reconceptualizing the nature of formal settings in which teaching and learning take place. In addition, we are developing alternative models for teaching and learning. We have rediscovered the importance of the home, parents, and peers in the educational process. And, we are experiencing rapid change and continual advances in the technology of teaching and in the definition of the goals, objectives, and products of education.

The broad concern with the process of education has created new audiences for education-related courses, a demand for new offerings, and the need for increased flexibility in the format for courses. Furthermore, colleges and schools of education are initiating new courses and curricula that appeal to the broad range of undergraduates and that focus squarely on current and relevant social and educational issues.

The Basic Concepts in Educational Psychology series is designed to provide flexibility for both the instructor and the student. The scope of the series is broad, yet each volume in the series is self-contained and may be used as either a primary or a supplementary text. In addition, the topics for the volumes in the series have been carefully chosen so that several books in the series may be adopted for use in introductory courses or in courses with a more specialized focus. Furthermore, each of the volumes is suitable for use in classes operating on the semester or quarter system, or for modular, in-service training, or workshop modes of instruction.

Larry R. Goulet

PREFACE

Psychologists and teachers share a common interest in understanding the thought and behavior of children. The theoretical issues that challenge the research psychologist often parallel the practical questions that challenge the classroom teacher. This book is designed to present psychological findings and theories in a way that emphasizes their practical significance.

Psychologists are intrigued, for example, by the inefficiency of young children's memory. Questions about the limits of young children's ability to remember and about the procedures that help them to remember better are currently of great interest in developmental psychology. Psychologists are interested in these questions because information about children's memory provides a key to understanding how memory works in all human beings. Because their interests are primarily theoretical, psychologists do not usually consider the practical implications of their research findings. Teachers, however, are most immediately interested in the practical rather than the theoretical implications of psychological findings. They want to know whether procedures that have helped children to remember better in laboratory tasks can be adapted to help children remember better what they learn in the classroom.

We are psychologists, not educational theorists or teachers of young children. The literature we have reviewed comes primarily from professional journals in psychology. We have, however, surveyed a sample of the educational literature in order to provide some examples of classroom practices that are consistent with the implications of the psychological research. Additional suggestions have been contributed by classroom teachers who read the earliest versions of this book; others have been collected from the authors' experiences as frequent observers in preschool classrooms.

This book can serve as a text in a variety of courses in education and psychology. Since the book focuses on cognitive development in children aged 3 through 8, its most obvious use is in educational-psychology courses that include students specializing in preschool or early elementary education. We believe that the emphasis on brief and clear descriptions of practical applications makes the book particularly suitable as a stimulus for discussion among education students or practicing teachers. In addition, the thorough coverage of the psychological literature and the extensive references will provide students of psychology with a sound and readable introduction to major topics in cognitive development.

This text is based on a report, *Cognitive Development in Young Children: A Report for Teachers,* which was prepared by the authors for the National Institute of Education (grant number NIE-G-74-0058) and published by the U.S. Government Printing Office in 1976. The present version has been revised, updated, and reorganized for use as a college text.

The preparation of this book, as well as of the report on which it is based, has involved the collaborative efforts of many individuals. We wish to thank Colleen Chapman, Phyllis Haas, Patricia Melgard, Leo Musberger, and their colleagues for providing classroom teachers' reactions to preliminary drafts of the manuscript. We also thank Ellis B. Evans, Wendy C. Roedell, Ronald G. Slaby, Mildred E. Kersh, and Nancy Cook for their many helpful suggestions and contributions to various chapters.

We are grateful to Dennis N. McFadden of Battelle Institute for providing the first author with her initial opportunities to review and synthesize a part of the relevant psychological literature and to Mildred Thorne, Project Officer at the National Institute of Education, for her support and encouragement of our work.

Finally, the authors wish to thank Larry Goulet, series editor, Carol Falender, University of California, Los Angeles, and Freda Rebelsky, Boston University, for their insightful comments and helpful suggestions for revision of the text.

Nancy E. Jackson
Halbert B. Robinson
Philip S. Dale

CONTENTS

CHAPTER FOUR
MEMORY   37

CHAPTER FIVE
LOGICAL THINKING   47

CHAPTER SIX
SUMMARY: HOW CHILDREN CHANGE AND LEARN   69

COGNITIVE DEVELOPMENT
IN YOUNG CHILDREN

CHAPTER
ONE
INTRODUCTION

> When I was a child, I spoke like a child, I thought like a child, I reasoned like a child; when I became a man I gave up childish ways.
>
> 1 Cor. 13 : 11

Some developmental psychologists might question whether adults really do give up childish ways of thinking altogether (Bruner, Olver, & Greenfield, 1966), but few would dispute that young children characteristically speak and act in ways that reflect a mental organization different from that of adults.

Different attitudes and theoretical orientations underlie research into the development of children's language, perception, memory, and logical thinking (see, for example, Baldwin, 1967; Dale, 1976; Farnham-Diggory, 1972; Gibson, 1969). These separate approaches are reflected in the four main chapters of this book. Nonetheless, each of the chapters reinforces the argument that young children's thinking is, in its own way, as systematic and predictable as adults' thinking. Because a child's world view is predictable, it can be shared by adults, and this sharing can form the basis of more effective teaching.

PRACTICAL APPLICATIONS OF BASIC RESEARCH: SOME WORDS OF CAUTION

In this book, reliable research findings and well-supported theoretical arguments have been translated into recommendations for teachers, which are listed at the start of each of the four main chapters. These recommendations are illustrative; they are not the substance of the text. More important by far are the discussions in each chapter of the psychological findings supporting each recommendation. We hope that our consideration of these findings will stimulate you to develop your own ideas for creating learning experiences suited to the particular characteristics of the young children with whom you work.

Many teachers are skeptical of the need to revise their teaching methods as each new psychoeducational model comes into vogue. In general, this conservatism is justified. Nevertheless, we believe that basic research findings provide a rich source of ideas for teachers to consider as they evaluate and, in some instances, change their classroom techniques. The implementation of ideas from research should, however, be undertaken with several cautions in mind.

One hazard inherent in translating research findings to practice is the ever-changing nature of psychological "truths." What seems "true" at one point in time often becomes "false" when new information becomes available or a new theoretical perspective changes the interpretation of old findings. Thus, even though we have tried to maintain a moderate and, indeed, a cautious stance in reviewing the psychological literature, we cannot be certain that some of the conclusions we have reached will not be revised or invalidated by future research. We have therefore limited ourselves to recommendations that are well grounded in common sense, as well as supported by empirical evidence. Any of the practices that we suggest may ultimately prove less effective than some alternatives, but none of them should interfere seriously with a child's learning and development.

Not only is psychological "truth" changeable, it also is for the most part probabilistic. In other words, most psychological findings are based on the behavior of *groups* of people. Techniques that produce small but reliable improvements in performance or that are associated with superior performance in a majority of cases can be fascinating to a psychologist, who is primarily interested in understanding the basic processes that govern behavior. To a classroom teacher, however, a very small improvement in performance might not justify the effort necessary to adopt a new method. More important, since the behavior of specific individuals does not always conform to the behavior that is typical of the group, it is quite possible that some or all of the children in a particular classroom might learn at least as well in circumstances that research indicates are "inferior" as they would in "superior" circumstances.

Age-stereotyping provides a good example of the dangers involved in relying too much on generalizations about groups. Psychologists and teachers both tend to group children by age and to assume, for example, that 6-year-olds, or first-graders, are relatively homogeneous in their abilities and interests. We are uncomfortable with generalities of this sort. Our professional experiences have included extensive contact with children who are exceptional in one way or another—children who have impaired hearing or language disorders, children who are mentally retarded, and children who are mentally advanced far beyond their years. We are well aware that any statement that contrasts, say, 5-year-olds with 7-year-olds ignores the probability that each of these age groups contains individual children whose behavior in some way or another fits the norm for the contrasted group. We have used such generalities in this book only because of the nature of the available information. We hope, however, that you will interpret these generalities in the light of what you know and observe about the behavior of particular children.

OBSERVING THE LEARNING PROCESS

Classroom teachers are in an excellent position to judge the effectiveness of various teaching techniques. Every classroom provides a unique combination of circumstances, and the standards for rating the success of an educational experience vary widely among schools and communities. However, whatever the characteristics of the class and the criteria for success may be, teachers who are careful observers of the learning process can judge for themselves the extent to which their goals are being realized.

Observing the classroom learning process is not easy. Teachers are handicapped by the differences between their own perspective and that of the children, as well as by the challenges that face anyone who wishes to make objective, reliable, and systematic observations of a complex situation.

Observations tend to be colored by what the observer expects to see and hear. It is often difficult to separate the events that we have actually observed from the inferences we attach to those events. For example, a teacher who sees that a young child habitually fidgets during group lessons should not immediately assume that the child is "hyperactive" or that the lessons are too difficult for the child to follow. Either of these inferences may be correct, but it is also possible that the child is unusually knowledgeable and consequently is bored by the simplicity of the lessons. Or perhaps the child has an undetected hearing or vision problem. The teacher who separates observation (the child fidgets) from inference (the child is hyperactive) is able to weigh all of the possible explanations for the observed behavior.

Objective observation is particularly difficult when the observer is also a participant in the process being observed. We all like to think that we are doing our work well. This natural bias can trap the teacher-observer into concluding that all of the children in the class are enjoying an experience when, in reality, the apathy of the majority is being masked by the enthusiasm of a few. Desire for success can also create the illusion that a child is making fewer errors this week than last or that the class is responding better to a new curriculum.

Teachers can employ a variety of simple strategies to become better observers and better judges of what is happening in their own classrooms. Keeping written records makes it easier to be objective and reliable. Simply making a note that a child was silent during Wednesday's discussion, spoke twice on Thursday, and made five remarks on Friday helps to keep accurate track of that child's progress. A written record is not subject to the distortions and deletions that wishful thinking can impose upon unaided memory.

Another great help to the teacher-observer is any opportunity to step back from involvement with the class for a few minutes to look at the total activity of the group. Observing oneself on videotape provides an excellent opportunity for constructive self-evaluation. When videotaping is not possible, a teacher may wish to exchange with a colleague the favor of observing in each other's classes. A nonparticipant observer has more time to observe the children, both individually and as a group, and thus is able to get a more comprehensive idea of how each child and the group as a whole are reacting to an experience. Moreover, the visitor's observations are somewhat less likely than the teacher's to be biased by the conviction that a technique recommended by the textbooks and carried out by a competent teacher must be working well.

The teacher's own systematic observations can provide information about any aspect of the social or intellectual atmosphere of the class, but they are particularly valuable as a source of information about the cognitive maturity of the children and the extent to which they share the teacher's perspective of a learning experience. For example, a child might be observed to insist that the amount of clay in a snake the child has made is greater when the snake is elongated than when the same snake is pounded into a pancake. Noting this logical "error" provides the teacher with information about that child's readiness for certain learning experiences in science and mathematics (see Chapter 5).

In this book, we give a description of young children's intellectual functioning. Our hope is that awareness of how the world is likely to appear from a child's point of view will help teachers to gain new insight into what is happening in their classrooms. We offer some theories about how young children think and some suggestions for teaching techniques that are consistent with these theories, but we defer to you to be the final judge of what works best in your classroom.

CHAPTER TWO

LANGUAGE

DIGEST OF RECOMMENDATIONS

1. *Suggested Teaching Technique:* Give young children ample opportunities to play and talk with one another and with adults.

   Rationale: Learning language involves talking as well as listening. Children talk a great deal when playing among themselves. Some children will talk fluently to their peers but not to adults.

   Selected References: Dale, 1976; Garvey & Hogan, 1973; Labov, 1970; Mueller, 1972.

2. *Suggested Teaching Technique:* Create situations in which children want and need to formulate clear and complete verbal messages. When they have difficulty with this task, help them by asking probing questions ("What else did it look like?" "What did you do then?") and by providing examples of good messages.

   Rationale: Children provide more complete verbal information when they know the listener really needs this information. Children who are ineffective communicators can improve with help and practice. Children tend to imitate the speech style of their teachers.

   Selected References: Flavell, 1967; Gleason, 1972; Peterson, Danner, & Flavell, 1972.

3. *Suggested Teaching Technique:* Provide children with extended exposure to the meanings of words such as *more, on, before,* and so on, in a variety of contexts. In your own use of these words, check to make sure that the children are understanding the meanings you intend.

   Rationale: Young children often understand only part of a word's full adult meaning. Children may mask the limits of their verbal comprehension by guessing meaning from the situation in which a word is used.

   Selected References: Cazden, 1972; Clark, 1973b; Thomson, 1972; Weikart, Rogers, Adcock, & McClelland, 1971; White, Day, Freeman, Hantman, & Messenger, 1973.

4. *Suggested Teaching Technique:* Provide examples of good English in your own speech, but resist the impulse to nag children about their grammar.

   Rationale: Children's grammar reflects a consistent, developing system that will mature without specific teaching. Children will imitate the speech patterns of teachers and friends whom they admire. Moreover, attempts to drill mature grammar into young children are fruitless and may alienate the children.

Selected References: Brown, 1973; Dale, 1976; Smothergill, Olson, & Moore, 1971.

5. *Suggested Teaching Technique:* Learn to understand and accept as legitimate the grammar and pronunciation of children who speak nonstandard English.

Rationale: Pressure doesn't succeed in changing the language patterns of young children. Children can understand and read standard English without speaking it, and nonstandard English is perfectly adequate as a tool for thinking and communication.

Selected References: Burling, 1973; Hall & Freedle, 1973; Labov, 1969, 1970.

6. *Suggested Teaching Technique:* In teaching reading to all children, but particularly to children who speak nonstandard English, emphasize comprehension rather than standard English phonetics. Adapt phonics lessons in spelling and reading to the pronunciation used by the children in the class.

Rationale: Emphasis on standard-English phonetic reading may lead to anxiety and failure. The ultimate goal of reading instruction is to enable individuals to understand what they read. Pronunciation is an intermediate step that can be handled in any dialect.

Selected References: Burling, 1973; Goodman, 1975; Labov, 1970; Smith, 1975.

7. *Suggested Teaching Technique:* Don't assume that children from disadvantaged backgrounds are "nonverbal" or that they lack the verbal skills necessary for thinking.

Rationale: Language helps children to think, but it is not a necessary tool for logical reasoning. Children from low-income families perform quite well on some measures of verbal ability. Verbal ability in nonstandard English is just as sufficient for thinking as verbal ability in standard English. The language children use in talking to a teacher may reveal only a fraction of their true competence.

Selected References: Cazden, 1972; Genshaft & Hirt, 1974; Labov, 1970; Shriner & Miner, 1968; Spence, 1973.

HOW CAN TEACHERS ENCOURAGE CHILDREN TO TALK?

Children learn to talk well (and, perhaps, gain a good foundation for writing well) by getting extensive experience in talking. Listening to a teacher is only part of language learning. To master a growing vocabulary and to develop ncreasingly mature ways of putting words together, children need to talk as well as to listen (Cazden 1972; Dale, 1976). Everyone likes to talk to people who respond. Classroom teachers are inevitably drawn to the most verbal children. As a result, quiet and inarticulate children become relatively more so as the school year progresses, while the teacher devotes more and more time to conversation with the children who probably need it least. One advantage of highly structured language-drill programs is that they ensure that all children get at least some experience in talking with the teacher (Cazden, 1972; Cazden, Baratz, Labov, & Palmer, 1972).

Certain teacher-child situations are better suited than others for getting the child to talk. As a start, the teacher can become a better listener by sitting or stooping to meet children at their eye level. Many children are turned off by teachers who ask questions that are tests of knowledge rather than real requests for information. A teacher who holds up an object and asks "What is this?" is asking a "test" question. The children know that the teacher doesn't need that information and is only testing their knowledge. Some children love such challenges; others avoid them with "I dunno" (Labov, 1972). Children seem to talk best when they can talk with a teacher and answer real questions in situations that are interesting to both the child and the teacher (Cazden et al., 1972). For example, rather than asking a child what he or she had for breakfast, a teacher might say to whoever is near and will listen "There are so many good things to eat for breakfast. I like orange juice. I wonder whether everybody likes orange juice" (Thomson, 1972, p. 23). This ploy is not limited to use in conversations about children's personal experience. We have observed a talented kindergarten teacher lead a lively and thought-provoking discussion about dinosaurs by interjecting such questions as "I wonder how the people who made this book knew what color to paint the dinosaurs?" The answer was not directly apparent but required that the children recall and apply knowledge about protective coloration learned several weeks previously. It was, in a sense, a "test" question, but the teacher's expression of her own puzzlement and her willingness to accept a variety of responses took the sting out.

The teacher's responses to children's speech are important in several ways. When teachers show their interest in what children say and refrain from turning a conversation into a grammar lesson, children are likely to talk more in the future. The teacher's language also serves as a model for children to imitate in their own speech. In one research study, preschoolers' speech was found to reflect their teacher's speech style after a few weeks of exposure to a particular style (Smothergill et al., 1971).

Some children do not talk well in the presence of a teacher, despite great efforts to engage their interest and to put them at ease. Some of these children come from backgrounds where it is not acceptable to speak at length to adults.

These children may, however, speak very well when they are given the opportunity to talk to other children (Dale, 1976; Labov, 1972). The quantity and quality of children's speech may vary with the types of activity in which they are involved. There is some evidence, for instance, that preschoolers talk to each other more while playing house than while playing with blocks or working on a craft project (Dale, 1976). Such data should, however, be interpreted with caution. Almost any group activity can stimulate conversation if the teacher has this goal in mind and provides materials or ideas that will facilitate discussion and cooperation (Thomson, 1972).

HOW CAN TEACHERS HELP CHILDREN TO USE LANGUAGE FOR EFFECTIVE COMMUNICATION?

Most of children's speech is intended to communicate a message, even though the actual communication may be rather inefficient. There are times, however, when children say things that are not intended for any listener. A child involved in a project might make remarks such as "That's a good one" or "Now I have to put one over here." Adults also mumble to themselves, of course, but children are more likely than adults to use "egocentric" speech when other people are present and to speak aloud rather than to mutter or speak the words silently.

Young children's egocentric speech is not an undesirable thing. It is a normal and useful stage that may be involved in the development of thinking and self-control (Conrad, 1971; Dale, 1976; Vygotsky, 1962). Moreover, egocentric speech accounts for a relatively small proportion of children's speech, even at the preschool level. Most of children's utterances have a clear communicative intent and are successful in eliciting some response from the listener (Garvey & Hogan, 1973; Mueller, 1972).

Even though much of young children's speech is not egocentric in *intent*, it may be egocentric in effect, in that it fails to provide all of the information needed by the listener. Consider the following interchange (Haas, 1974):

> *Teacher (seeing Jimmy looking dejected):* What's the matter?
> *Jimmy:* I can't find it.
> *Teacher:* What can't you find?
> *Jimmy:* The big one.

Much of what a young child says can be understood only if the listener can see what the child sees or remembers the past event the child is trying to describe. Preschool speech relies heavily on tone of voice, pointing gestures, and the use of indefinite pronouns; a 3-year-old, for example, will say "What is it?'' to a listener in the next room who couldn't possibly know what ''it'' is (Krauss & Glucksberg, 1970).

Young children fail to communicate clearly in large part because they do not understand what the listener needs to know and what they must say to provide that information. They produce their best efforts when the needs of the listener are dramatic and obvious—when, for instance, a child is asked to describe a set of materials so that a blindfolded listener can perform some task. Even when children perceive the listener's needs, however, they may give less-than-adequate information, particularly if the ideas to be communicated are complex (Flavell, 1967; Maratsos, 1973b).

Learning to use language well involves developing the ability to appreciate the needs of the listener and to provide complete *verbal* information. The need for such a skill will be particularly critical when a child begins to communicate in writing, because the gestures and intonation that amplify the message of oral language cannot be incorporated into written language.

There are a number of strategies that teachers can use to help preschoolers and early elementary school children communicate better. One important strategy is giving children opportunities to take turns as both speaker and listener. Several curriculum packages, borrowing from research methodology, suggest structured ''communication games'' in which a child must convey information to another player who cannot see what is being talked about (Bartlett, 1972). For instance, two children might sit at a table on which a screen has been placed to block their view of each other and of each other's sections of the table. Each has an assortment of shapes with which to make a design. The children take turns as speaker and listener. The speaker makes a design with the shapes and then tries to describe the design so that the listener can make an exact copy.

Four-year-olds who are initially poor at these games become competent talkers after a few weeks of playing the game with an adult who asks leading questions and provides a good example of how the game should be played. One child initially tried to identify a picture for another ''blind'' child by saying ''People are sitting next to each other.'' After four weeks of training, the child described the same picture as ''the picture with a cat and a mother who's holding the cat and telling her baby to pat it, I guess'' (Gleason, 1972, p. 105).

Communication skills can also be taught in the course of everyday classroom activities. For example, children can be asked to convey oral messages to a teacher or child in another room or to describe an ongoing activity to someone who has just joined the group. Adult listeners or bystanders can help the young messenger by probing for any information the child has omitted.

The kind of help children need to improve their attempts at communication depends on their age. Children 7 or 8 years old will improve an inadequate message in response to vague hints from the listener, such as ''I don't understand.'' Preschoolers need more detailed help and should be asked specific questions, such as "What else does it look like?" "What color is it?" or "What did you do next?" (Flavell, 1967; Peterson, Danner, & Flavell, 1972). Children at any age profit from the combined experience of trying their own communications and listening to teachers' examples of clear and complete messages. Improvement in young children's communications skills does not, however, rely solely on experience in conversing with adults. There is some evidence that children communicate more effectively and less egocentrically when talking among themselves than when talking with adults. One possible interpretation of this observation is that peers are ideal communication partners. Unlike an adult, a playmate listener is very similar to the child who is speaking, making it easier for the speaker to infer what the listener wants and needs to know. At the same time, a playmate lacks the adult's tolerance and ability to cope with ambiguous or incomplete information. Young children demand—and apparently get—each other's clearest communication efforts (Piaget, 1959).

HOW DO CHILDREN LEARN THE MEANINGS OF NEW WORDS?

Learning the full adult meaning of words is a complex process that is not complete until well into the elementary school years. With the exception of proper names, words always refer to *categories* of objects or events. To learn a new word, a child must learn the extent of the category to which it applies. This learning requires extensive experience with a word in the greatest possible variety of applications and contexts.

Most early-childhood programs stress the learning of particular sets of vocabulary words that will ultimately be useful in learning situations. Many of these words deal with relationships of quantity, space, and time or with dimensions of objects. The "cognitive code" vocabulary of many preschool programs includes words such as names for colors and shapes, *more, less, big (bigger, biggest), small (smaller, smallest), between, behind, on top of, beside, before, after,* and so on (Bartlett, 1972; Cazden, 1972; Weikart, McClelland, Hiatt, Mainwaring, & Weathers, 1970; Weikart, Rogers, Adcock, & McClelland, 1971). These words are involved in the description or directions that accompany many early learning situations, and it makes sense to ensure that children learn them.

The "cognitive code" words are often difficult to learn because they express ideas that require children to attend to an unchanging feature or relationship (*red, bigger, on top of*) that must be separated from the individual situation in which the word is used. Children must learn that all sorts of objects can be *red*, that there are a whole range of colors that can all be called *red*, that a thing that is *bigger* than a breadbox may not be *bigger* than a house (Dale, 1976). Since learning these word meanings involves a gradual sorting out of properties, children's learning is best facilitated by opportunities to encounter new words in a variety of situations, both verbal and practical. Children need to deal with *more* and *less*, for instance, in cases of discrete, countable quantities and of continuous, fluid quantity. They need to learn that if one thing is *more*, then another is *less*, or that sometimes two quantities are *the same*. Children also need to hear words used in a variety of sentence contexts so that they can appropriately separate the meaning from the context. For instance, a child who hears sentences such as ''Before you close the door, turn out the lights'' has to learn the meaning of ''before'' in the difficult language context in which the order of the words is different from the order of the sentence meaning.

Having a child hear or say a word in a single, repeated situation will not help the child to learn the full meaning of the word in the range of situations to which it must ultimately be applied. A better way for children to learn the meanings of new words is suggested by Thomson:

> When one is planning a ''language experience'' it is easy to narrow the activity to materials that are specifically designed for the acquisition of specific language skills. This may be very appropriate. However, language is an activity that invades every portion of the preschool program, and therefore a teacher is providing language experiences in each activity and in each portion of the day in which she is responsible for interaction with children. Thus, while a teacher may plan an activity to enable children to acquire a certain skill, she might also look for a variety of ways and times throughout the day when acquisition of this skill can be emphasized. For example: suppose a teacher plans a specific game where she cues children to place cereals in different positions on an object; an activity to teach the comprehension of prepositions. She might consider other times during the day to emphasize preposition comprehension: clean-up time when she might tell children where to place materials or ask children where they placed them; washing hands before snacks when she might ask children who is in front of Billy, behind Jane, beside Joe, etc. . . [pp. 134−135].*

Many of the most difficult words for young children to understand are those whose comprehension requires abstract reasoning ability or familiarity with subtle conventions of language use. For instance, an adult might look at a person and, judging from gray hair, stooped posture, or other cues, decide that the person could be described as ''old.'' In choosing this word, the adult is relying on knowledge that these perceptual cues are fairly reliable signs that a large number of years have passed since a person's birth. The adult's word choice might also reflect the specific context of the remark. An ''old'' graduate student, for instance, might be considerably less stooped and gray than an ''old'' professor.

Young children's word usage sometimes reveals their lack of mastery of

*From *Skills for Young Children*, by C. L. Thomson. Copyright 1972 by Carolyn L. Thomson. Reprinted by permission.

the subtleties that govern adult usage. Preschoolers, for instance, call a human figure "older" if it is *larger* than a comparison figure, even though such other cues as dress and body proportion clearly contradict this usage (Kratochwill & Goldman, 1973; Looft, 1971). Young children are also prone to use words in inappropriate contexts, occasionally amusing adults with such statements as "There's only a small piece of cake, but it's middle-aged" (Chukovsky, 1968, p. 3). Adults' own language usage is frequently of little help to children who are in the process of sorting out the rules for using a particular word. A preschool child who confuses "older" with "bigger" is showing the influence of listening to adults who use "big" as a synonym for "old," "grown-up," or "mature." The adult who uses "big" in this way knows that "big" does not always imply "old," but a young child is less aware of the full meanings of the words and can therefore be misled into inappropriate usage.

Despite occasional errors in children's speech, it is often difficult to tell when a child's understanding of word meaning differs from an adult's. Young children have usually mastered some aspect of a word's meaning. This incomplete understanding may serve children sufficiently well most of the time, but children with incomplete understanding can have difficulty when the teacher's use of words and their own interpretations don't coincide. Many psychological research techniques have been designed specifically to lead children into errors in word comprehension or usage in order to reveal the limits of understanding that might not surface consistently in real-life situations (Donaldson & Balfour, 1968; Donaldson & Wales, 1970; Maratsos, 1973b, 1974).

"More" and "less" are good examples of words that are imperfectly understood in the preschool years. Children aged 3 or 4 seem to understand that "more" and "less" are related to the dimension of quantity, but they have not yet sorted out the differences among "more," "less," and "the same amount." "More" seems to be understood earlier than "less," and there is a period during which children seem to think that "less" means the same as "more" (Donaldson & Balfour, 1968).

Antonyms in general are difficult for young children to sort out, which is not surprising, since opposites such as *more/less, before/after,* and *big/little* really share almost all of their meaning. *Hot* and *cold,* for example, both refer to extremes of temperature, *before* and *after* to a relationship between non-simultaneous events (Clark, 1972).

Children can often respond correctly to verbal directions even when they are not paying attention or are unable to understand what is said. Children (and adults in similar circumstances) do what they think the speaker wants, judging from the circumstances. If a teacher says "Put the crayons ———— the box," a young child, seeing a box at hand, will put the crayons inside the box and will probably be correct. Children below the age of 3 will often put an object inside a container even if the direction is to place the object *under* or *on* the container. On the other hand, a child who faces a table or other large object with a flat surface will assume that the direction is to put the crayons *on* the table (Clark, 1973b). In familiar situations, children often act more on the basis of past experience with what is expected than on the basis of the verbal instructions actually given, particularly if they cannot understand what the teacher is saying. Such guessing is not undesirable; it is, in part, the way in which children learn new word meanings and grammatical patterns. Teachers should be careful, however, in assuming that children understand a word because they appear to comprehend it in a particular situation. A child has not fully understood a word until he or she has sorted out the features that distinguish it from words of similar meaning and has grasped the word's meaning in the full range of situations to which it might be applied.

One way in which children's understanding of words improves as they grow older is from a limited understanding of the word in a specific context only ("on" applies to things with surfaces but not to containers) to a broader, more flexible understanding (Clark, 1973a, 1973b). Teachers who know the limits of children's understanding can talk with children in ways that they can understand. Knowing "where a child is" also permits the teacher to present words in ways that will help expand the child's understanding to more mature levels.

SHOULD TEACHERS TRY TO "IMPROVE" YOUNG CHILDREN'S GRAMMAR?

Child: Nobody don't like me.
Teacher: No, say "Nobody likes me."
Child: Nobody don't like me. (8 repetitions of this dialogue)
Teacher: No. Now listen carefully. Say "Nobody likes me."
Child: Oh! Nobody don't *likes* me! (McNeill, 1966, p. 69.)

Every teacher or parent has tried to do something about a child's persistent errors in speaking and has been frustrated by the child's failure to respond to direct preaching about grammar. Adults can sometimes produce changes by providing a model of correct speech and rephrasing the child's utterances in adult form, but this technique produces immediate results only if the child is ready to imitate the change. Otherwise, the benefits of speaking correctly to children are to be seen only over a period of weeks, months, or years. The child in the example above was ready to adopt the standard-English rule that calls for "s" to be added to a verb in the third person singular but was not ready to abandon use of the double negative (McNeill, 1966).

Children's grammar is difficult to change because it is not simply bad speaking or a mishmash of random errors. Children talk in the way that they do because they have their own grammar, which makes perfect sense to them; it just happens to be slightly different from adult grammar (Dale, 1976). The differences between child and adult grammar tend to be particularly noticeable when children make errors such as the following:

"Nobody don't like me."	Double negative; lack of subject-verb agreement.
"She holded them loosely."	Overgeneralization of "ed" as past-tense ending.
"All the childrens came."	Overgeneralization of "s" as plural ending.
"Why you don't come?"	Failure to change word order in forming question.
"Her did it."	Wrong case of pronoun.

When children make these kinds of errors, they are not necessarily reproducing the kind of language that they've heard at home or at school. They are merely speaking in an immature system of their own, and their speech will change in time. A young child's grammar is, at any stage, a reflection of the child's best current guess about the structure of his or her native language. The "guesses" are constantly changed and improved as the child matures (Brown, 1973).

Although there is little reliable information concerning ways in which teachers and parents might help a child's grammatical development, it does seem that giving children a chance to talk a lot themselves and to hear adult speech is the natural and perhaps the only way for development to proceed. Adults sometimes like to repeat what children say in an expanded and corrected form. This tendency is natural and it may be helpful in the long run. Children should not, however, be required to rephrase their own statements. As in the example above, expecting children to imitate grammar too far from their own levels leads to repeated failures and frustration for both teachers and children (Cazden, 1972; Dale, 1976). Given ample opportunities to speak and to hear adult language, children will eventually master mature forms of their native language.

An additional consideration for teachers of children who speak non-standard dialects is that dialect speakers sometimes use grammatical forms that appear to be immature forms of standard English but that are actually based on mature rules of nonstandard English. The double negative, for instance, is a perfectly legitimate, rule-governed form in Black-English vernacular as well as in many foreign languages (Labov, 1972). Furthermore, the double negative of Black-English vernacular is governed by grammatical rules different from those that govern the primitive double negative used by very young children who are learning standard English (Brown, 1973). *Children who speak nonstandard English are not, for that reason, speaking a grammatically immature or deficient*

language. Children's grammar must be evaluated in terms of the language or dialect that they are acquiring (Dale, 1976).

HOW CAN TEACHERS WORK EFFECTIVELY WITH CHILDREN WHO SPEAK NONSTANDARD ENGLISH?

A large number of American children come to school speaking languages other than the standard English that is officially and socially acceptable in White middle-class society. Some of these children come from homes in which a foreign language, such as Spanish, is spoken. Others speak regional or racial dialects of English that are different enough from the standard to cause problems of communication and social prejudice. We will focus here on the group of dialects known as Black-English vernacular, because they have been studied more extensively than other nonstandard forms, and because some form of Black English is the language of a large proportion of school children.

The Black English spoken by many inner-city children differs from standard English in its vocabulary, pronunciation, and grammar (Labov, 1972). Vocabulary differences present relatively little difficulty in the classroom. Children learn to use certain words and not others when talking to teachers, and teachers learn to comprehend the children's special vocabulary. The differences between Black and standard English in rules for pronunciation and grammar do often lead to problems in school, however (Labov, 1970, 1972). The differences between the dialects in underlying linguistic rules are relatively minor, but the resulting differences in word sounds and sentence structure can lead to considerable misunderstanding.

One problem for the child who speaks any nonstandard dialect is the prejudice that some teachers may feel against someone whose speech does not conform to standard. The child's language may be classified as "retarded" or "restricted," and the child may be thought to be stupid. This prejudice is completely unreasonable. There is no evidence that any language is, as a whole, better or more complex than any other language (Langacker, 1973). In comparing two systems, one typically finds that one dialect makes elaborate distinctions in one area, the other in different areas. Black English, for example, distinguishes between an activity occurring a single time and an activity that is habitual or repeated. "He working" corresponds to "He is working right now," whereas "He be working" means "He usually works" or, perhaps, "He has a steady job" (Labov, 1969). Any language can be used well or badly for communication. In evaluating communication skill, it is often necessary to overcome prejudices about style in order to focus on the meaning of the message.

Simply eliminating social prejudice against the various forms of nonstandard English would not erase the difficulties inherent in maintaining a school system for children who come from a diversity of linguistic backgrounds.

Because the various dialects of English are much more similar than they are different, educational programs have in the past tended to rely completely on materials that are appropriate for speakers of standard English, without any consideration being given to the complexities that certain activities might raise when some or all of the children in a classroom speak varieties of nonstandard English. Consider, for instance, the lessons often used to acquaint children with English spelling and sound patterns. Children are often asked to find sets of words that rhyme with one another. Teachers whose classes include children who rhyme *pour* and *more* with *sew* cannot make rhyming into a useful lesson unless they work from the pronunciation rules that the children are using as well as the rules in textbooks of standard English (Burling, 1973).

There is no reason why children who speak nonstandard English should not be able to pronounce words in their own way and at the same time learn to write using standard spelling. English spelling is a difficult and erratic system regardless of the dialect used to pronounce it, and all children are faced with the task of learning many spellings by memorizing individual words and special patterns. Teachers who are sensitive to children's pronunciation rules and who refrain from imposing their own are likely to have much greater success than teachers who lack this flexibility (Burling, 1973; Labov, 1970, 1972).

Dialectal differences in grammar and pronunciation complicate the learning of reading for both children and teachers. Although several alternative methods, such as reading instruction using dialect materials, have been tried in recent years (see Dale, 1976, for a review), most children who speak Black English are still given reading instruction from materials written in standard English.

Teachers of children who speak Black English sometimes insist on standard phonetic reading of standard-English materials, treating as errors any deviations from the standard pronunciation of what is printed. When this approach is used, the dialect-speaking child is at a consistent disadvantage to the child whose own speech more closely follows the patterns of the text. The dialect speaker must learn a new way of talking at the same time as he or she is learning how to read. The anxiety aroused by this difficult task may eventually discourage a child from trying to read (Goodman, 1975).

An alternative approach advocated by some psychologists and linguists is to permit children to read standard materials in their own dialect (Burling, 1973; Dale, 1976; Labov, 1970, 1972). It does not seem to be very difficult for Black-English speakers to translate automatically from the standard English of the printed page to their own dialect. The dialects are sufficiently similar that the meaning of a passage is rarely affected by this process. The "errors" that occur during the translation are analogous to the minor changes that all fluent readers make as they move quickly through a passage. Skilled reading is dependent not on a fixed and arbitrary decoding of printed symbols to spoken sounds but on a transmission of information on the page to understanding in the head.

Thus, a fluent Black reader might properly read "He always looked for trouble when he read the news," as "He a'way look' fo' trouble when he read (rhyming with *bed*) de news." The meaning of the sentence loses nothing in the translation. Permitting Black-English-speaking children to read standard materials in their own dialect is probably much easier for them than insisting that they use standard English in reading aloud. This procedure does, however, place a considerable burden on the teacher who is not thoroughly familiar with the rules of Black English. The teacher must know how to distinguish changes that represent correct translation from changes that reflect deficiencies in a child's understanding of the material. For example, a rendition of "read de news" in which "read" rhymed with "seed" would indicate a failure to pick up the past-tense cue in the main verb (Labov, 1970).

The reluctance of many teachers to accept Black-English pronunciation and grammar from children probably stems from the feeling that, when such a procedure is followed, the children are not learning about standard English. However, speaking and understanding are somewhat separate aspects of language development. Children can learn to read or listen to standard English with comprehension without producing standard pronunciations and grammatical forms in their own speech. Even though efforts to drill standard usage into young dialect speakers are probably doomed to frustration and failure for a complex of linguistic, psychological, and sociological reasons (Burling, 1973; Dale, 1976; Labov, 1972), these children apparently have no difficulty in comprehending the standard-English speech or writing of others. There is abundant evidence that they comprehend and remember standard English just as well as they do their own dialect and just as well as do children who speak standard English (Anastasiow & Hanes, 1974; Copple & Suci, 1974; Frentz, 1971; Genshaft & Hirt, 1974; Hall & Freedle, 1973; Johnson, 1974).

Many strategies suitable for teaching reading to all children are particularly relevant for children who speak nonstandard English. Teachers might wish to consider the following:

1. Emphasizing the importance of reading and writing as communication tools. For instance, children can be given "important" messages to decipher, such as "The snack is in the closet" (Goodman, 1975).
2. Using reading materials that reflect the patterns of the children's own speech, such as literature written in dialect or the children's original compositions (Burling, 1973; Labov, 1970, 1972; Smith, 1975).
3. Stressing reading for comprehension rather than standard-English phonetic pronunciation. The traditional practice of having children read aloud for the teacher can be supplemented by silent reading followed by group discussion

of the material or by individual work on comprehension exercises, such as connecting words and pictures (Burling, 1973; Dale, 1976; Smith, 1975).
4. Encouraging, rather than discouraging, children's attempts to guess words from contextual clues as well as from the form of the word. Guessing from context is a common practice among fluent adult readers. The practice may be especially helpful to children who, because of nonstandard pronunciation, find "sounding out" particularly difficult (Dale, 1976; Smith, 1975).
5. Adapting phonics instruction to the pronunciation used by the children being taught (Burling, 1973; Labov, 1970, 1972).

This discussion of Black-English vernacular is intended only as a brief introduction to the issues involved in designing educational programs for our multidialectal culture. Psychologists and linguists have made extensive studies of dialectal differences and of the nature of language itself. These studies provide detailed information to help teachers understand how dialects differ, what the differences mean, and how school experiences can be adapted to cope with these differences. Even teachers who are fluent speakers of both nonstandard and standard English can profit by learning how the dialects are related and why old-fashioned rules of "proper" language are largely nonsense. Particularly concise and comprehensible treatments of this subject are listed at the end of this chapter.

IS LANGUAGE TRAINING AN EFFECTIVE WAY TO IMPROVE CHILDREN'S ABILITY TO THINK?

A number of popular preschool programs, the best-known being Bereiter and Engelmann's DISTAR program, place heavy emphasis on language drill as a way of teaching a child to talk "better" and to *think* "better" (Osborn, 1968). Drill sessions involve the participation of small groups of children and a teacher in a series of set routines. For instance, a teacher might hold up an object and say "this is a cup" or "this is a car." The children are asked to repeat the teacher's statements in unison, matching the teacher's exact pronunciation as closely as they can. The drill might then proceed to an exchange of questions (from the teacher) and answers (from the children), such as "Is this a ball?" (holding up a car), "No, this is not a ball" (Weikart, McClelland, Hiatt, Mainwaring, & Weathers, 1970). In their original conception, language-drill programs were based on the following set of related assumptions:

1. The ability to use language is critical for logical thinking.
2. Preschool children from low-income backgrounds have inadequate language skills and are therefore poorly equipped for thinking.
3. Language skills, and consequently thinking, can be improved by concentrated drill in stereotyped patterns of response.

Is the ability to use language critical for logical thinking? This question is by far the most complex of the three. The answer depends on precisely how one looks at the question. The acquisition of language does influence and enhance children's thinking in a number of ways. When a child is able to link up understanding of a situation with the use of the right language, the child achieves a high level of control over that situation.

In learning names for objects, children are forced to attend to the features that most reliably distinguish one object from other objects with different names. As names for sets of things are learned, the similarity among things with the same name (for example, trees) and the difference between things with different names (trees versus telephone poles) become more obvious. Learning language thus helps children to perceive experiences in adult ways (Gibson, 1969; Reese & Lipsitt, 1970).

Children who have learned names for dimensions and relationships are perhaps better equipped than other children to solve problems on the basis of classes and relations rather than individual instances. For example, a child who knows the word "bigger" and learns to solve one problem by always choosing the "bigger" thing is likely to apply the same verbal rule to similar problems. Children may sometimes achieve the same results without using language, but language is certainly no hindrance (Cole, 1973; Cole, Gay, Glick, & Sharp, 1969; Spence, 1973).

Learning language, and learning to *use* language, also expands the potential of a child's memory. The ways in which language can help children to remember are discussed in Chapter 3.

Another way in which the acquisition of language might influence thought has received little research attention and so is a matter of speculation. Learning language may itself be the most impressive intellectual feat accomplished by young children. In the first few years of life, usually without any formal instruction, children learn an enormous set of words and sounds and a complex system of grammatical rules. The "push" given to children's thought processes by the demands of language learning may well carry over to other areas of cognition.

In discussing the relationship between language and thought, psychologists often stress the *limits* of the influences of language on a young child's behavior and argue that not until age 5 or 7 does a child use language for thinking. Nonetheless, preschool children can and do act and think in many ways that rely on their verbal skills. They can, *within limits,* follow verbal directions, communicate verbally to others, absorb ideas from verbal presentations, and think creatively on a purely verbal level. One preschooler, for example, asked her mother why pigs were not milked. Her mother replied "They have little ones to feed." The child countered with "So do cows have calves—try again, Mommy" (Blank, 1974), thus demonstrating an ability, shown by most young children at some time or another, to think logically in a situation in which the "problem" and the "solution" are entirely verbal. The difference between young children and older children or adults is not the presence or absence of the ability to use language for thinking but the *range of situations* to which this ability can be applied and the *efficiency* of its application (Blank, 1974).

Although learning language does expand the possibilities of children's thinking, it may be more accurate to emphasize that children's language *reflects* their intellectual growth (Sinclair-de Zwart, 1973). In many situations, a child's nonverbal understanding precedes and surpasses the ability to use the relevant language. For instance, 4- and 5-year-olds understand the *concept* "big" correctly, even though they confuse the *word* "big" with the word "tall" (Maratsos, 1973a).

Developing language helps children to think, and developing new ways of thinking helps children to learn language. Young children who have been virtually without language are, however, less pervasively handicapped than one might expect from the discussion above. Deaf preschoolers who have not yet learned sign language are able to cope fairly well with tests of logical-reasoning ability (Furth, 1971; Spence, 1973). Thus, although language is an aid to thinking, it is not an absolute necessity.

Do young children from low-income backgrounds lack sufficient language skills for logical thinking?   If language does help children to think better, even to a limited extent, children with serious language deficiencies might be expected to have difficulty in thinking and learning. Psychologists and educators have therefore wondered whether the academic difficulties that are common among children from low-income families might be traced to deficiencies in their language development.

The degree to which low-income children appear to be linguistically deprived depends to a great extent on how their language skills are measured. During the 1960s, estimates of the language skills of children from low-income families suggested that these children suffered from massive language deficiencies—massive enough, perhaps, to be a source of problems in thinking (Bernstein, 1961; Osborn, 1968). These early estimates were made, however, by researchers who had no understanding of the nature of dialectal differences and who judged children's "deprivation" largely in terms of the degree to which their language failed to conform to middle-class speech patterns. These estimates also failed to allow for the tendency of many low-income children to become suddenly nonverbal when tested by a strange adult (Burling, 1973; Labov, 1972).

More recently, psychologists and educators have pointed out that most "nonverbal" children speak fluent, complex, and effective language when they are among themselves or away from school. In addition, the language skills of children who speak nonstandard English are much more impressive if their language is evaluated by its own rules, which are the only sensible measure (Burling, 1973; Cazden, 1972; Labov, 1972).

Tests of children's ability to comprehend and manipulate the grammatical structure of language find no racial or social-class differences in children's performance (LaCivita, Kean, & Yamamoto, 1966; Shriner & Miner, 1968). These studies supplement the evidence, reviewed in the previous section of this chapter, supporting the competence of lower-class, non-White children in understanding both their own dialect and standard English. Both middle- and low-income Black children are actually more skillful in language tasks than in tests of reasoning, arithmetical skill, or spatial-conceptualization ability (Stodolsky & Lesser, 1967).

Thus it appears that there is no massive deficit in the language competence of children from low-income homes. They may sometimes have particular difficulty in performing some of the language tasks required in school, and they may need some extra help in specific areas, such as mastering the "cognitive code" vocabulary (Cazden et al., 1972; Gleason, 1972). There is no evidence, however, that these children suffer from a general lack of "thinking language."

In summary, there is no reason to suspect that commonly observed socioeconomic-class differences in general conceptual ability are the result of a specific deficit in language skill.

Will language drill help a child to think better?   Language-drill programs have been popular because they have frequently been successful in producing relatively large, fairly enduring gains in school performance and test scores (Osborn, 1968; White et al., 1973). This success could be taken as support for the philosophy that language drill trains "good thinkers." However, there are other facets of the programs, such as the high degree of teacher-child contact and the development of skills that will make the child popular with teachers, that might account for the results. Indeed, a general pattern in compensatory-education literature is the finding that programs with specific goals, a detailed curriculum plan, high teacher-pupil ratios, extensive teacher-child interaction, and enthusiastic staff are successful regardless of the particular flavor of the approach used (White et al., 1973).

Children in language-drill programs do learn how to speak confidently and how to answer teachers' questions in acceptable form. The system can be defended for its accomplishments, but, as the previous sections have shown, there is little reason to suppose that the success of language-drill programs can be attributed to improvement in *thinking* as a result of children's learning of a limited set of words and expressions in a rigid, repetitive format. Furthermore, some of these programs may do a long-term disservice to children by restricting their opportunities to practice the language they already know in relaxed conversation with their peers and teachers.

Points to Remember

The preceding discussion of language development can be summarized in a few general principles that have direct relevance in classroom procedures:

1. Children get useful language practice by talking and listening to one another.
2. Children talk when they want to communicate and when they know that the listener wants to hear what they have to say.
3. Young children often have difficulty in formulating clear and complete messages that can be understood without reliance on nonverbal cues. Practice, with helpful suggestions and examples provided by the teacher, can improve their performance. Practice in communication with other children may also help children to become less "egocentric" in their speech.
4. Children's grammar is a logically consistent, developing system that will mature in time without specific teaching during the preschool and primary years.
5. Children learn new word meanings by a long, slow process of experience with words in a variety of practical situations and sentence contexts. Some words require considerable logical sophistication to be fully understood.
6. The language of children who speak nonstandard English is perfectly adequate for communicating and for thinking. Children can learn to read and understand standard English without learning to speak that dialect.
7. The problems that low-income children sometimes have in school cannot be traced to lack of a "thinking language."

Recommended Reading

Burling, R. *English in black and white*. New York: Holt, Rinehart and Winston, 1973.
Dale, P. S. *Language development: Structure and function*. New York: Holt, Rinehart and Winston, 1976.
Labov, W. *The study of nonstandard English*. Champaign, Ill.: National Council of Teachers of English, 1970.

CHAPTER THREE
PERCEPTION

DIGEST OF RECOMMENDATIONS

1. *Suggested Teaching Technique:* In every learning situation, consider the possibility that children might not be attending to those aspects of the situation that an adult would notice.

   Rationale: Perceptual development is in large part a process of learning to recognize which features or dimensions of a complex situation are most important.

   Selected References: Gibson, 1969; Pick, Frankel, & Hess, 1975.

2. *Suggested Teaching Technique:* Help children learn how to direct their attention by giving clear and consistent feedback on the correctness of their work.

   Rationale: In laboratory learning situations, indication that each of a succession of choices is right or wrong helps a child to identify the relevant dimensions of a problem.

   Selected References: Pick et al., 1975; Reese & Lipsitt, 1970.

3. *Suggested Teaching Technique:* Simplify learning situations as necessary to highlight the significant features of problems.

   Rationale: Young children are easily distracted by irrelevant information and may have difficulty in searching a complex perceptual situation for the most important features.

   Selected References: Miller & LeBlanc, 1973; Pick & Pick, 1970.

4. *Suggested Teaching Technique:* Design lessons so that the information presented is neither completely strange nor completely familiar, but just at the edge of the children's experience and ability to comprehend. Prepare children gradually for unusual experiences or difficult concepts.

   Rationale: Children are most likely to attend to and learn from activities that build on and expand their previous experience and understanding.

   Selected References: Kagan, 1972; Piaget, 1951.

5. *Suggested Teaching Technique:* Plan group learning experiences so that they can be grasped by individual children on a variety of levels.

Rationale: Different children of the same age may differ in their sophistication to such an extent that some members of a class are bored by a lesson because it is too easy while others are bored because it is too difficult.

Selected References: Weikart, Rogers, Adcock, & McClelland, 1971.

6. *Suggested Teaching Technique:* In preparing children for learning to read, stress activities, such as rhyming, that involve listening to the sounds that make up a word.

Rationale: Detecting the sound components of words is likely to be difficult for young children. First-graders who are good at tasks such as rhyming tend to be good readers.

Selected References: Gibson & Levin, 1975.

7. *Suggested Teaching Technique:* When children have difficulty in making a particular type of discrimination, such as distinguishing between *b* and *d* or between *m* and *n,* create learning situations that highlight and contrast the features that distinguish the confusing forms from each other. Teach children to use the names for the items to be discriminated.

Rationale: Practice in discriminating and naming the actual forms a child must learn is the type of activity most likely to help the child learn particular discriminations.

Selected References: Flavell, 1970; Gibson & Levin, 1975.

In some school tasks, such as reading, the perceptual component is obvious and has been the subject of considerable educational research and theorizing (Gibson & Levin, 1975). Understanding of the extent of children's ability to discriminate and interpret sensory information is, however, as relevant to the teaching of mathematics, tricycle riding, and social skills as it is to the teaching of reading. Whatever the subject matter, children's learning is affected by the nature of the information that their senses are taking in, and this information may be quite different from what an adult would perceive in the same situation.

HOW DOES SENSORY DISCRIMINATION IMPROVE WITH AGE?

In a way, children's discrimination abilities are functioning adequately from infancy onward. Infants and toddlers are quite capable of relatively fine discriminations among visual patterns, colors, musical tones, and speech sounds (Cohen & Salapatek, 1975). Children's sensory systems do change slightly as they mature, but these physiological changes have little impact on perceptual capacity in most real-life situations (Pick & Pick, 1970).

Everyday learning situations, however, require much more than the sensory capacity to detect a difference between two isolated events. Discrimination in the broad sense, or perception, is a process that draws on all of a child's intellectual skills and previous experience. Perception is most challenging for young children when a quick response is called for, when perceptual information is incomplete, when critical information is buried in a mass of extraneous detail, or when a series of events must be perceived as a unit (Goodnow, 1971; Hartley, 1976; Pick & Pick, 1970; Potter, 1966).

As children grow older, they remember better, acquire the ability to organize information in terms of language and abstract concepts, and develop more mature logical-reasoning skills. All of these achievements are intimately related to age changes in perceptual ability. The key to this relationship appears to be the process of selective attention.

WHAT DOES IT MEAN FOR A CHILD TO "PAY ATTENTION"?

Attention is the process of tuning in to sensory information. Attention is highly selective; human beings typically ignore much of the great mass of stimulation impinging on their senses at any given moment. Thus, the distinction between a child's total environment and the attended-to, effective environment may be critical for an understanding of the child's behavior.

We often assume that children are "paying attention" if they are sitting quietly and looking in the direction of whatever we want them to see or hear. Such common-sense behavioral estimates of attention can be very useful, and they have been employed in psychological research as well as in everyday situations (for example, see Cohen & Salapatek, 1975; Kagan, 1971). However, a child's appearance is not always a good indication of whether, or to what, the child is attending. Teachers often report cases like that of Alison, a 3-year-old who regularly chooses not to participate in preschool "music time," spending this period playing alone in another corner of the room instead. Despite her apparent inattention, Alison obviously learns a great deal from music time, for she delights her mother by singing the many new songs that she has learned at school (Haas, 1974). Children can and do take in information without appearing to pay attention. They are also quite capable of giving the appearance of rapt interest without mentally tuning in to the information they need in order to learn from a classroom experience. A noisy, squirming, or apparently apathetic child may, in some cases, be attending more effectively than a model pupil.

In general, the psychological-research literature suggests that rewarding children simply for "paying attention" is less likely to lead to efficient learning than is creating situations that draw the children's attention to the critical features or dimensions of a problem (Pick et al., 1975).

WHAT FACTORS CONTROL A YOUNG CHILD'S ATTENTION?

The direction and duration of a young child's attention are difficult to predict in the complex environment of the classroom, but there are a few principles, derived from children's behavior in simplified laboratory settings, that should apply in any situation.

A first premise, one that is obvious yet often ignored in practice, is that children will not attend to information they cannot discriminate. A habitually inattentive child should always be checked for possible impairment of hearing or vision.

Given that children are able to see and hear what is happening, a second principle is that the events most likely to capture their attention are those that have acquired some meaning for them through past association with important consequences. In large part, age changes in perception can be attributed to learning where to look, or how to listen, for the critical features of a situation (Gibson, 1969; Pick et al., 1975).

We have all had the experience of suddenly hearing, above a general hubbub of conversation, the sound of our own names being mentioned. Our attention is captured by that sound, even though it is no louder than the rest, because it has a personal significance. In any complex situation, the features that are the most meaningful to us are the ones that stand out.

A major task facing children during their early school years is learning what features of situations are important for them to attend to. For example, beginning readers need to learn that the size and color of written symbols are unimportant but that their shape, spatial orientation, and sequence convey critical information.

The way in which children learn to isolate the critical features of classroom experiences is probably analogous to the process children go through in solving the multidimensional discrimination problems presented in laboratory studies of learning. In a typical discrimination-learning problem, a child is presented with pairs of objects or pictures that vary in several dimensions: a large red circle, for instance, might be presented together with a small blue square. The child is asked to indicate the ''correct'' form and is rewarded with a candy or token for appropriate choices. On the first trial, even the child who guesses correctly has no way of knowing which aspect of the chosen stimulus makes it ''the right one.'' The large red circle might be correct because it is large, because it is red, or because it is a circle. However, as the learning session progresses, the child is shown many different stimulus pairs representing various combinations of objects that vary in size, shape, and color. By a process of trial and error, the child eventually learns that, for instance, *size* is the critical dimension in this particular problem—the larger member of any pair always being the correct choice (see, for example, Reese & Lipsitt, 1970).

In these laboratory learning situations, it is vital that children receive clear and consistent feedback on the correctness of their choices. Reward and punishment, such as a "yes" for a correct choice and a "no" for an incorrect choice, give children the information they need to direct their attention appropriately and to solve the problem. In the laboratory, rewards have been found to work best when they direct a child's attention to the appropriate features of the problem at hand. Sometimes a highly attractive reward, such as candy, interferes with learning by distracting the child's attention from the task itself (Spence, 1970).

Laboratory studies of learning have also demonstrated the value of children's learning and using names for patterns or events that must be discriminated. The learning of names for particular categories of experience requires an ability to isolate and attend to the distinctive features that identify one group and distinguish it from similar groups (Flavell, 1970; Pick & Pick, 1970). For example, in order to apply the appropriate verbal labels to various pictures of dogs, cats, and horses, a child must have a clear idea of the features that reliably distinguish these four-legged creatures from one another. As we pointed out in the previous chapter, it *is* possible for children to have mastered a concept without knowing the corresponding verbal label; however, mastery of the label ensures the child's formation of the category, at least to the extent that the child gives the name the correct meaning. Furthermore, the child's act of producing the name often has a direct, positive effect on learning.

Even though classroom learning situations are typically more complicated than those that are created in the psychological laboratory, the same principles can be applied to teaching children how to attend appropriately. There is evidence, for example, that young children learn better when a teacher's instructions are brief and to the point than when the instructions include information that is not essential for learning the task (Miller & LeBlanc, 1973). Beginning students cannot be expected to have sufficient insight to know which parts of a teacher's instructions are important and which can be safely ignored.

We have noted that young children often attend to different features of a situation from those that an adult would attend to. For this reason, there are many occasions when children may be trying to solve a problem that is quite different from the one the teacher thinks has been posed, sometimes even giving the right answer for the wrong reason. How this "generation gap" influences children's learning of word meaning is discussed in Chapter 2.

The "generation gap" in perception occurs in other contexts besides the learning of word meanings. For example, materials that are color coded to "help" a child learn to discriminate differences in number or length may actually complicate the problem by distracting the child from the critical dimension (Schell, 1971). Piaget (1971) has suggested that the color coding of Cuisinaire rods can sometimes make it more rather than less difficult for children to learn the number and length relationships that the materials are designed to teach.

Piaget predicts that color coding should be minimally distracting when the rods are actively manipulated by the children themselves (as they were designed to be) and the length and number relationships naturally highlighted, but that color coding will be *more* distracting when the rods are used for demonstrations by the teacher, with the children watching but not participating.

The simplification of learning situations to highlight critical features can be overdone, however. Young children do need help in sorting out the important and unimportant features of learning situations, but oversimplification may lose their attention by making the situation too simple and therefore boring. Children tend to be interested in experiences that are just complicated and challenging enough to stretch the limits of their current understanding without overwhelming them.

Research with infants and young children supports the argument that children are most attentive to events that are slightly different from what is familiar and expected (see, for example, Kagan, 1971, 1972; Piaget, 1952). With age and experience, every child builds up a repertoire of expectations about how things should be. Human faces, for instance, are expected to have two eyes, one nose, and a mouth in the usual arrangement. When these expectations are violated, as in the distortions and dismemberments often suffered by cartoon characters, young children are fascinated. Depending on the child and the circumstances, this fascination may be accompanied by horror or by delight. Sometimes children are frightened by experiences that are a bit too strange for them to understand. For example, consider the following reaction of a group of preschoolers to a new experience:

> The young 3-year-olds at their group table had mixed reactions to a hand puppet of a dog used for helping the children increase and focus their attention. All of them focused directly on it, three of them with smiles. Tammy and Timmy did not want to touch it. They pulled back their hands and shrieked. The following day, when the puppet was used at the next table, another 3-year-old, Paula, responded in a similar way [Weikart, McClelland, Smith, Kluge, Hudson, & Taylor, 1970].

If Tammy, Tommy, and Paula had had no idea at all of what the puppet was, they would probably have ignored it rather than have been frightened by it. Evidently they understood enough to know that a moving, disembodied animal head was not ''normal,'' but not enough to know that it was a safe toy. When children react in this way to a strange experience, the teacher can help them to gradually understand the experience, so that it will no longer be frightening. The children in this example might overcome their fear of the puppet through a sequence of lessons about their own bodies and body parts, the body parts of a doll, the making and manipulating of puppets, and the difference between real and toy dogs (Weikart, McClelland, Smith, et al., 1970).

The strong impact of unusual events is not limited to sights or sounds that violate a child's expectations about surface appearances. Similar power is exerted by any experience that tests and extends a child's conceptual understanding of the world and how it works. If a new experience is totally unrelated to what a child already understands, the child may ignore or avoid the experience, just as an adult who is not a scientist would tune out a technical lecture on nuclear physics.

According to cognitive theory (Piaget, 1971; Weikart, McClelland, Smith, et al., 1970), children are naturally drawn to comprehensible but challenging experiences and will attend to them without any external rewards or threats. However, the children in a class are likely to show considerable variation in their readiness to master a particular concept. This diversity can make the planning of group learning experiences very difficult. Some children may be bored because a lesson is too simple at the same time as others in the group are bored because it is too difficult. Often the most successful group lessons are those that can be appreciated on a variety of levels. For example, a demonstration of magnetism involving iron filings, paper, and several differently shaped magnets is fun for children who are interested only in the apparently magical movements of the filings as well as for those who are able to abstract some understanding of the physical laws governing the movements.

In summary, children do not always pay attention to those aspects of a situation that interest adults. When this discrepancy interferes with learning, the teacher can help by simplifying the perceptual situation and by giving the child consistent information about what features of the situation are important. Most children, however, don't need external rewards in order to maintain a general interest in learning new skills and ideas. Experiences that are challenging but within a child's powers of mastery or comprehension have an innate power to catch and hold the child's attention.

HOW DOES CHILDREN'S ABILITY TO CONTROL THEIR ATTENTION CHANGE WITH AGE?

The burden of structuring a learning situation so that children will attend appropriately rests most heavily on the teacher whose pupils are very young. As children grow older, they become much better able to direct their own attention as required by the demands of a particular task.

One limiting factor in very young children's ability to control their own attention is their inability to plan and carry out a coordinated search for useful information. This inability is often obvious when a preschooler is asked to search for a misplaced object. There may be a flurry of energetic activity, but it is unlikely that the child will move systematically through all of the likely locations. Between the ages of 3 and 7, children's ability to control their attention in the conduct of a search improves dramatically.

Young children's difficulties in finding missing objects are paralleled by the difficulty they have in searching for a particular detail of a picture or printed word. Comprehending a complex visual pattern requires more than a single glance. To learn what is in the pattern, children must move their eyes purposefully, scanning the various parts of the pattern. Studies in which children have been asked to identify, match, or discriminate among objects have found that older children are slower and more accurate in their judgments (Abravanel, 1970; Pick & Pick, 1970; Potter, 1966; Zaporozhets, 1965). They are also more efficient in their search; they act as if they know where to look for critical information (Nodine & Lang, 1971). Given a concealed object to identify by touch, 6- or 7-year-olds trace the object's outline with their hands, but 3- or 4-year-olds grasp it in their palm without manipulating it systematically (Zaporozhets, 1965). With more experience (usually between ages 7 and 9), children also learn when to stop attending. Younger children continue to search a pattern long after discovering the information necessary to solve a problem, but older children stop searching as soon as they find the answer (Bruner, Olver, & Greenfield, 1966; Pick & Pick, 1970).

To some extent, improvements in search skills probably reflect children's learning of how to recognize the aspects of an event that are most likely to be important. In complex situations, however, there is also the influence of developmental changes in children's ability to plan and regulate their behavior. Older children are capable of forming and carrying out a search strategy that scans the most likely spots first, covers the remaining alternatives, and ceases when no more information is necessary (Pick & Pick, 1970).

As children grow older, they also become increasingly able to tune out irrelevant information. Preschoolers' attention is captured by any intense, recognizable, or puzzling event. If something is naturally intriguing, few preschoolers are able to ignore it on command (Johnson, Warner, & Silleroy, 1971; Odom & Guzman, 1972). For this reason, young children are often said to be "distractable." A voice from the playground may intrude on what the teacher is saying; the sight of another child's interesting activity may draw attention away from a half-finished project. Preschoolers tend to notice bits and pieces of everything they are exposed to. Older children and adults become very efficient at attending only to those elements that are relevant in a particular situation. Since young children often do not distinguish between what they need to know and what is incidental, they attend to, and learn, a little bit of everything, rather than concentrating efficiently on the essentials of a problem (Hagen, 1972; Lehman, 1972; Maccoby & Konrad, 1967; Pick et al., 1975).

Preschoolers are not totally unable to control their attention. Over time, they do learn how to attend in standard situations that occur often enough to provide them with the opportunity to learn appropriate habits (Gibson, 1969). Sometimes they may attend and learn better if they are instructed to remember specific things (Yussen, 1974). They are also quite able to block out monotonous and uninteresting distractions, such as the clatter of a typewriter (Turnure, 1971).

Young children may also find it difficult to attend simultaneously to several aspects of a situation. Although it might seem paradoxical, the increase with age in children's ability to focus attention is accompanied by an increased ability to "decenter" and consider several aspects of a problem simultaneously. There is no actual conflict, of course, in saying that children's attention becomes both more focused and less "centered" as they mature, since these abilities relate to different aspects of perception. As children grow older, they learn to focus on important information; they also learn that certain situations require simultaneous attention to more than one factor.

Until about age 8, for example, children are likely to say that a tall, thin glass contains more to drink than a short, fat glass, even though the shorter glass actually contains the same or even a greater quantity. They center their attention on one dimension, the height of the liquid, and ignore its width (Curcio, Kattef, Levine, & Robbins, 1972; O'Bryan & Boersma, 1971; Piaget, 1968). Depending on one's theoretical viewpoint, this behavior may seem to be more of a logical than an attention problem (Gelman, 1969; Piaget, 1968). However, there is evidence that children as young as 4 can coordinate attention to two problem dimensions if both dimensions are high in salience—that is, are readily noticed (Odom, Astor, & Cunningham, 1975). Whatever the reason, young children do tend to notice that particular aspect of a problem that is most obvious and to try to solve the problem without attending to and considering other factors. This propensity may be partly responsible for young children's tendency to make impulsive and erroneous judgments on perceptual problems: they fail to attend to and weigh all of the evidence (Hartley, 1976; Katz, 1971).

Children who work slowly and accurately at perceptual problems are described as "reflective"; those who work rapidly and less accurately are described as "impulsive." As children grow older, they generally seem to become more reflective and less impulsive (Kagan, 1971; Katz, 1971; Meichenbaum & Goodman, 1971). They become more able to sit still and to study problems thoroughly before making a decision. There are undoubtedly many situations that call for a quick response on the basis of the most prominent features of a situation. In many classroom situations, however, slow and careful judgments are more likely to be correct than hasty responses. Children who are habitually more impulsive than their peers may sometimes have difficulties in learning. Some impulsive children have become slower and more accurate workers after going through a carefully planned program designed to help them focus their attention on the specific requirements of a task.

Working with a group of unusually impulsive 8-year-olds, Meichenbaum (Meichenbaum & Goodman, 1971) required children to talk to themselves about how to solve a problem. The children first watched a teacher demonstrate "self-directing" speech and then were encouraged to imitate the teacher's behavior while tackling the task on their own. The children were taught to remind themselves of the requirements of the task, of the need to work slowly and carefully, and of the need to correct errors rather than to give up. For example, a child might be encouraged to mutter the following:

> Okay, what is it I have to do? You want me to copy the picture with different lines. I have to go slow and be careful. Okay, draw the line down, down, good; then to the right, that's it; now down some more and to the left . . . that's okay. Just erase the line carefully. . . . Good. . . . Even if I make an error I can go slowly and carefully . . . [Meichenbaum, 1971, p. 18].

Big Bird has demonstrated this technique in some episodes of *Sesame Street*.

Another approach for helping impulsive children learn better is based on evidence indicating that their difficulty is not that they respond too quickly but that they fail to attend to all aspects of a problem. Hartley (1976) found that impulsive and reflective first- and fifth-graders were equally accurate in solving problems in which the relevant dimension was easily noticed. Reflective children were more accurate than their impulsive classmates only on problems in which the relevant dimension was not obvious. Impulsive children were not any quicker in their responses to these problems, but they were less thorough in their search for information.

Hartley's data suggest that the most helpful training for impulsive children is training that stresses the importance of noticing all of the features of a problem. Other researchers have demonstrated the effectiveness of such training in improving impulsive children's problem-solving accuracy (see Hartley, 1976). However, it is possible that different training techniques might work best for different children and that the technique best suited to improving a child's performance on one type of task will not be equally effective for another type of task. As is so often the case, teachers who wish to apply psychological-research findings in their classrooms should plan their own evaluation of what procedures are most helpful to a particular child with a particular learning difficulty.

WHAT PERCEPTUAL PROBLEMS ARE INVOLVED IN BEGINNING TO LEARN TO READ AND WRITE?

As they grow ready to read and write, children learn to discriminate the component sounds of spoken language, to identify and produce the visual forms of written language, and to match sounds with their corresponding written symbols.

For most beginning or soon-to-begin readers, learning to hear the sound patterns within words presents some difficulty. According to Gibson and Levin

(1975), preschoolers do not spontaneously notice the individual sounds, or phonemes, that make up a word. Teachers can informally evaluate children's ability to analyze words into component sounds by noting how well they succeed at games requiring them to think up rhymes or words that correspond in initial sound. First-graders who do well at such games tend to be better readers than first-graders who do not. Although this relationship does not prove that practice in rhyming will make good readers out of poor ones, it does suggest that rhyming and other activities that direct children's attention to sound patterns within words are relevant to reading and may help prepare children to read.

Learning to identify and produce the letter forms of written language seems to come easily for most children. It may take some time for preschoolers to learn to identify their letters. After the first grade, even poor readers are well able to identify single letters (Shankweiler & Liberman, cited in Gibson & Levin, 1975).

Many preschool programs devote considerable time to training letter discrimination by requiring children to feel sandpaper letters or to trace letter forms. The theory behind these activities is that motor practice in following the forms of the letters will transfer to and facilitate the child's ability to identify the letters by sight. The theory is a reasonable one, but the available evidence strongly suggests that children learn to discriminate letters at least as well when they can concentrate on looking as when their training involves tracing or other motor activity (Williams, cited in Gibson & Levin, 1975). It may be that, for most children, motor practice unnecessarily complicates an essentially simple learning problem.

Although children evidently don't have to write in order to learn how to read, practice in writing naturally helps them to learn to write. This practice can be quite informal and unstructured. Given opportunities to write and an array of models to copy, kindergarteners gradually progress from scribbling to conventional printing of letters and words. Improvement occurs without interference or correction from adults. Apparently, kindergarteners enjoy having opportunities to practice writing and are able to check and correct their own efforts against standards available in the classroom (Wheeler, cited in Gibson & Levin, 1975).

While the discrimination and production of letters and letter combinations generally seems to present little difficulty to beginning readers, many children do have difficulty, sometimes well into the primary grades, in handling two particular features of written forms: letter orientation and letter sequence. Orientation errors, such as confusion of *b* with *d* or *m* with *w*, often persist well after children have mastered most other letter discriminations (Harris, 1972). Even more persistent are errors involving letter sequence. Among kindergarteners, reversals in letter order account for most of the errors made in picking a match for a sequence such as *CO* from a set of alternatives including the choices *OQ, OC, QC, CQ* and *CO* (Calfee, Chapman, & Venezky, cited in Gibson & Levin, 1975). Even in the third grade, poor readers may have difficulty in making correct matches for strings of letters (Shankweiler & Liberman, cited in Gibson & Levin, 1975). Young children's attention to the features of letter orientation and sequence may be facilitated by practice in exercises focusing on forms with contrasting orientations, such as *b* and *d*, or contrasting sequences, such as *rat* and *tar*.

As children begin to read and write, they learn to integrate their perception of the components of speech sounds with their perception of written language. Some psychologists have suggested that a child's readiness to begin reading is determined by the development, as the child matures, of a general ability to coordinate information between different sensory channels. Tests of auditory-visual-integration ability have been proposed as predictors of reading readiness or reading achievement (Birch & Belmont, 1965; Muehl & Kremenak, 1966). However, there is convincing evidence that the ability to integrate information from several senses is present from infancy onward (for example, see Bower, 1971). Furthermore, intersensory matching tasks are not necessarily more difficult for young children than are comparable tasks within a single sense modality (DeLeon, Raslan, & Gruen, 1970; Goodnow, 1971; Jones & Alexander, 1974; Kuhlman & Wolking, 1972). Thus, it is not surprising that the relationship between children's reading ability and their performance on such intersensory tasks tends to be too low to have practical diagnostic value (Reilly, 1972).

Matching the visual patterns of written language to the sound patterns of spoken language is not an easy task for most children, but the difficulty lies in the fact that they are *different systems* rather than in the fact that one pattern is auditory and the other visual. To translate from one system to the other, children must abstract the critical features of each and establish a whole set of correspondences. For example, beginning readers must understand that the spaces between strings of letters on a printed page indicate breaks between words. While many children acquire this understanding without any specific classroom instruction, some first-graders are unaware that spaces between printed words separate units of meaning (Meltzer & Herse, cited in Gibson & Levin, 1975).

The child's mastery of the system of written language seems to be facilitated by the same propensity to perceive and use general rules that guides the development of oral language (see Chapter 2). Children do not learn letter-sound correspondences in a tedious, instance-by-instance manner but rely on spelling rules that can be applied to generate many different words. General rules are, of course, the essence of phonics instruction. However, at least some children seem to make up their own phonics rules well before the time when they are exposed to the adult system. These "spontaneous spellers" (Read, 1971) write using a consistent, rule-governed system that shows a clear developmental progression. Forms commonly produced by spontaneous spellers are often quite different from the standard forms. For instance, "married" might be written as "mared," "helped" as "halpt," or "circus" as "srkis." These spellings may appear idiosyncratic to an adult, but long-term study of a number of spontaneous spellers has indicated that these children have analyzed the sounds of oral language and systematically translated them into a written form that is quite as logical as the standard spelling.

Children who start out with their own spelling systems do not seem to have any difficulty in making the transition during the primary grades to more standard spelling rules. A teacher who appreciates a child's independent achievement of a personal spelling system can help the child to understand how the standard system differs from the child's own.

Several general recommendations can be derived from the psychological literature on how children master the perceptual components of reading and writing. Preschool and primary programs probably err more often in the direction of overemphasizing perceptual training than in neglecting it. Many children master the perceptual components of reading and writing without any specific training. Difficulties are most likely to occur in the analysis of sound patterns within words and in the discrimination of letter sequences. The learning experiences most likely to prevent or overcome such perceptual problems are those that direct children's attention to the critical features of a situation.

Points to Remember

1. No one perceives all of the aspects of a complex situation, and young children may attend to different features of a situation from those that an adult might notice.
2. "Paying attention" is not necessarily synonymous with sitting quietly and looking at the teacher. The best measure of children's attention to a lesson is whether the children can demonstrate mastery of the information presented.
3. Young children often need to learn which features of a situation are important to learning or which aspects of a problem must be considered in order to respond appropriately. Teachers can help children to attend appropriately by simplifying the perceptual aspects of beginning lessons and by giving children consistent feedback on the correctness of their responses.
4. Children may be bored by experiences that are insufficiently challenging as well as by experiences that are too difficult to comprehend. Since children in a class vary greatly in their sophistication with regard to any situation, the best group learning experiences are those that can be appreciated at several levels of difficulty.
5. Young children are less able than older children to maintain control of their own attention. They have difficulty in planning and carrying out a systematic

search for information, in focusing attention on relevant information only, and in coordinating simultaneous attention to several critical aspects of a situation. Given these limits, teachers of young children need to be sensitive to the perceptual components of learning situations.

6. Impulsive children may be helped to work more slowly and carefully through training in verbal control of their own behavior or through training that stresses thorough consideration of all problem dimensions.

7. Beginning readers are likely to encounter some difficulty in analyzing the component sounds of oral language, but learning to discriminate the forms of written language generally does not present a problem for them. Experiences helpful to beginning readers and writers include practice in rhyming games, unstructured practice in writing and copying letters and words, and practice in tasks that require attention to the sequence of letters.

Recommended Reading

Gibson, E. J., & Levin, H. *The psychology of reading.* Cambridge, Mass.: MIT Press, 1975.

Pick, A. D., Frankel, D. G., and Hess, V. L. Children's attention: The development of selectivity. In E. M. Hetherington (Ed.), *Review of child development research* (Volume 5). Chicago: University of Chicago Press, 1975.

CHAPTER
FOUR
MEMORY

DIGEST OF RECOMMENDATIONS

1. *Suggested Teaching Technique:* Present new information in small doses: the younger the children, the smaller the dose. Add more only after each dose has been well learned.

    Rationale: Young children have very limited short-term memory capacity and can absorb only a few items of new information at one time.

    Selected References: Farnham-Diggory, 1972; Goodnow, 1972; Miller, 1956.

2. *Suggested Teaching Technique:* Recreate experiences in words or pictures so that children can recognize material from past activities. Photographs or tape recordings of a field trip or special project will help children to remember what they did. Showing children the illustrations from a story will help them retell the story.

    Rationale: Young children have excellent perceptual-recognition memory. Preschoolers are almost as accurate as adults in recognizing things that they've seen before.

    Selected References: Berch & Evans, 1973; Brown & Scott, 1971; Fajn-sztejn-Pollack, 1973; Hoving, Morin, & Kronick, 1970; Perlmutter & Myers, 1974.

3. *Suggested Teaching Technique:* Repeat information as needed until children remember it well. One correct answer doesn't necessarily indicate enduring memory. Repetition can take the form of presenting the same information in a variety of contexts.

    Rationale: Children remember better if information is presented more than once. Repetition is helpful even when the same idea is presented in several different forms. Children who partially understand an idea are likely to maintain interest until they have fully mastered it. Repetition is a form of play for young children.

    Selected References: Brown & Scott, 1971; Hoving, Coates, Bertucci, & Riccio, 1972; McCarson & Daves, 1972; Millar, 1968. (See also Chapter 3.)

4. *Suggested Teaching Technique:* Permit children to become actively involved with the information they are to remember. Involvement may be built into observational learning—when children are asked to predict the

outcome of a teacher's actions, for example—or it may come when children work with materials on their own.

Rationale: Memory is often enhanced by activities such as talking or thinking about experiences or by actual physical involvement with concrete materials.

Selected References: Balling & Myers, 1971; Blank & Frank, 1971; Wolff, 1972; Wolff, Levin, & Longobardi, 1972.

5. *Suggested Teaching Technique:* Make sure children know the correct names for things. It is especially important to have preschoolers repeat the names *out loud* while learning.

Rationale: Labeling aloud helps young children to remember. Elementary school children may do this spontaneously and silently, but preschoolers need to be encouraged to label aloud.

Selected References: Flavell, Beach, & Chinsky, 1966; Kingsley & Hagen, 1969; Locke & Fehr, 1970.

6. *Suggested Teaching Technique:* Plan a series of lessons around the same theme; try to relate new learning to experiences that are already familiar and comprehensible to children.

Rationale: Information that is organized, familiar, and comprehensible is easier to remember.

Selected References: Hall & Halperin, 1972; Horowitz, Lampel, & Takanishi, 1969; Rossi & Wittrock, 1971.

7. *Suggested Teaching Technique:* Plan problems so that they don't demand too much of young children's short-term memory. Young children can sometimes handle more advanced logical problems if the problems don't require much use of memory.

Rationale: "Memory aids," such as writing down the terms of a problem, help elementary school children to solve problems that would be beyond them if they were given orally. Preschoolers do better at problems involving only a few elements.

Selected References: Balling & Myers, 1971; Roodin & Gruen, 1970. (See also Chapter 5.)

8. *Suggested Teaching Technique:* Teach children to *try* to remember. Children often remember better when they are taught to use tricks such as saying things over and over to themselves (verbal rehearsal), organizing information in logical groups, writing things down, or using pictorial "notes" to help themselves remember things. Preschoolers might participate in setting up pictures or diagrams to show where various toys are stored. Elementary school children could make drawings of a display that they have created and then use the drawings to set up the display on another day.

Rationale: By about age 6, children spontaneously begin to use memory strategies such as verbal rehearsal. Preschoolers often remember better when they are taught these strategies.

Selected References: Corsini, Pick, & Flavell, 1968; Kingsley & Hagen, 1969; Ryan, Hegion, & Flavell, 1970.

9. *Suggested Teaching Technique:* Use techniques that help memory even when children appear able to get by without this help.

Rationale: Children as old as 8 frequently remember better if they are given the aids suggested in this digest.

Selected References: Farnham-Diggory, 1972; Goodnow, 1972; Hagen, 1972.

WHAT ARE THE DIFFERENT TYPES OF MEMORY TASKS?

Parents and teachers of young children are often perplexed by the excellence of a young child's memory in some circumstances and the inadequacy of the same child's memory in slightly different circumstances. For example, the child who seems incapable of following a simple set of directions may astound adults by recognizing many details of a place last seen months or even years before. Such inconsistencies are less puzzling in the light of the different kinds of problems and behaviors that involve some type of memory. Young children are virtually as good as adults at some kinds of memory tasks, but they are very poor at others. How well children remember depends on factors such as whether short- or long-term memory is called for and the type of behavior with which a child is asked to show evidence of remembering.

Many psychologists categorize memory processes into two types. *Long-term memory* is the process whereby enduring records of experience are stored. An experience may be stored in the form of sensory images of what actually happened or in the form of verbal or symbolic translations of that experience. Once information is stored in long-term memory, it is probably there for a lifetime, but it may be inaccessible because it is somehow blocked by interference from other learning. Experiences that fit well with what children know already will be more systematically ''filed'' and thus be easier to recall.

The second process is *short-term memory.* This process provides for temporary storage both of new information and of well-known information that has been retrieved from long-term memory because it relates to what is happening at a given moment. The short-term ''storage chamber'' can hold only a very limited amount of information at one time. In adults, this limit is about seven ''chunks'' of information, plus or minus two (Miller, 1956). Seven chunks of information might be seven unrelated one-digit numbers or seven randomly selected words. When information is organized into meaningful patterns, as when a string of unrelated words is reordered into a sentence, the chunks become larger and the capacity of short-term memory increases dramatically.

Organization of information facilitates the use of both short-term and

:mory. In long-term memory, organization permits efficient filing retrieval of information. In short-term memory, organization in- formation-holding capacity of this limited-capacity processor. The auu.~.. 76 Oak Street,'' for example, is much easier for someone in the United States to remember than adjoining addresses would be, because the person trying to memorize it can, with the aid of information retrieved from long-term memory, remember the house number as a single unit by relating it to a well-known concept.

Children's success in remembering also depends on the way in which they are asked to remember. When children are asked simply to recognize whether an experience is familiar or new, they are usually quite accurate. Differ- entiating between familiar and unfamiliar events is an easier memory problem than verbally recalling or nonverbally reconstructing the past. Recognition requires only the matching of a perceptual event that exists in the present with an event that occurred in the past. Recall and reconstruction, on the other hand, require the rememberer to recreate a past event from a record that is stored mentally. How much easier it is to recognize that a face is familiar than to dredge up the name that should be associated with it!

In the pages that follow, it will become evident that young children's memory performances show patterns of strengths and weaknesses that are related to the type of response by which memory is measured, the meaningfulness and organization of the material to be remembered, the way in which information is coded for storage, and the pace at which new information is presented.

HOW IS YOUNG CHILDREN'S MEMORY DIFFERENT FROM ADULT MEMORY?

Memory is not an automatic, ''mindless'' process, but ''a special case of intelligent activity, applied to reconstruction of the past . . .'' (Piaget, 1968). The maturity of children's reasoning skills and the scope of their knowledge affect how well they will be able to remember, particularly when memory tasks require focusing on select samples of important information, organizing material into systematic units, or translating experience into efficient codes. A general rule is: the older the children, the better their memory skills. Performance on recall and reconstruction tasks has been shown to be better in children who are older, brighter, or more familiar with the type of information to be remembered (Flavell, Beach, & Chinsky, 1966; Hagen, 1972; Locke & Fehr, 1970; McCarson & Daves, 1972; Roodin & Gruen, 1970; Ryan, Hegion, & Flavell, 1970).

One exception to the general pattern of increasing memory skills with increasing age is the performance of young children in tasks of recognition memory. Children as young as 3 years old are amazingly accurate in their ability to recognize which of a large set of objects or pictures they have seen before and which are new. Young children perform almost as well as adults, even when there is a delay of days or weeks between the time they first saw the material and the time of the recognition test (Berch & Evans, 1973; Brown & Scott, 1971; Fajnsztejn-Pollack, 1973; Hoving, Morin, & Kronick, 1970; Perlmutter & Myers, 1974). Recognition of perceptual images may tap more elementary skills than are required for other types of memory tasks.

On the other hand, young children have a very limited ability to absorb and recall new information. They process few elements of new information at a time, and the few that are retained for a second or two are likely to be lost before they can be used. In the standard digit-span memory task, adults can recall a series of about seven numbers, but preschool children typically can cope with no more than 2 or 3 digits, 5-year-olds with about 4 digits, and 6- to 7-year-olds with 5 digits (Farnham-Diggory, 1972). In different tasks, the number of items a child can recall might differ. Whatever the task, short-term memory capacity increases as children mature (Goodnow, 1972; Haith, 1971; Sheingold, 1973).

Inexperienced teachers are often tempted to present too much information too fast. A preschool lesson on shape concepts may proceed well as long as the teacher restricts the discussion to "circle" and "square" but collapse when "triangle" is prematurely added to the set.

The limited capacity of their short-term memory affects not only children's ability to memorize but also their ability to follow instructions and to use remembered information in solving logical problems. Young children are often more successful at solving complicated problems if they are given memory aids that remove the need to remember all of the problem's components and the steps to its solution while working out the answer (Balling & Myers, 1971; Roodin & Gruen, 1970; Thurm & Glanzer, 1971). Older children and adults routinely use such memory aids as writing down complicated problems. Young children have a much greater need for such strategies but are much less likely to use them spontaneously.

The use of strategies for remembering distinguishes the memory performance of preschoolers from that of older children. Although there are reports of exceptions to this rule (for example, Yussen, 1974, 1975), in most research situations preschoolers do not remember any more effectively when they are told to do so than when no such instructions are given (Appel, Cooper, McCarrell, Sims-Knight, Yussen, & Flavell, 1972; Flavell, 1970). By age 5 or 6, children are much more likely to have and to use the knowledge that remembering is a task that requires special effort.

Organizing information in some systematic way is a very useful strategy for aiding recall. If children are specifically told to remember something, they may adopt this strategy. First-graders, for instance, are more likely to sort a set of drawings into logical categories when told they will be asked to recall the drawings than when they are instructed simply to look at them. In this situation, it has been shown that the instructions to remember and the activity inspired by the instructions increase the amount of information that children recall six weeks after seeing the material (Salatas & Flavell, 1976). Another approach for helping young children to organize information for better recall is to impose the organization after, rather than before, the information is presented. In one study (Williams & Goulet, 1975), preschool children were shown a set of pictures and then asked to name all of the items that they had seen, one category at a time. Prompting children to recall first all of the toys, then all of the fruits, and so on helped them to remember better than when they were free to recall the items in any order.

Sorting information into logical clusters is only one of several strategies older children and adults rely on when trying to learn and to remember new information. Another strategy, called *verbal rehearsal*, is often used when the information to be learned is verbal or can be readily labeled. Verbal rehearsal is simply the repetition of information, silently or aloud, from the time the information is originally encountered until the time it is either firmly fixed in memory or no longer needed. Although preschoolers have less extensive vocabularies than adults and thus may have more difficulty applying memorable labels to some events, they do label events for which they have a name—for example, by spontaneously naming each object in a picture book. However, even when preschoolers know the appropriate names for a set of items to be remembered, they do not repeat these names over and over in a verbal-rehearsal process (Flavell, 1970; Flavell, Beach, & Chinsky, 1966; Kingsley & Hagen, 1969; Locke & Fehr, 1970). Preschoolers and kindergarteners can be taught to label and rehearse out loud, and they usually remember better when they use these techniques. However, asking preschoolers to label and rehearse *silently* does not seem to help their memory performance.

When a memory task calls for a nonverbal response, such as recognition or nonverbal reproduction, nonverbal strategies may help children to remember. One approach that is often successful with adults and elementary school children is to ask the rememberer to concentrate on a perceptual image, keeping a picture or sound "in mind" after it has been removed. In one study, 4-year-olds were able to recognize three-dimensional nonsense shapes better when they were instructed to visualize the shapes than when they received no such instructions (Millar, 1972). In other studies, however, instructions to form images have not been particularly helpful to young children (Reese, 1973; Robinson & London, 1971).

Since young children recognize a familiar experience more easily than they can recreate it in their own words, recognition tasks can be used to prompt more complete memory. For instance, a child who cannot retell a story without help will probably recognize the illustrations and may be able to use them as cues for organizing recall of the story. Teachers can also build on children's recognition memory by beginning new lessons or activities with a summary of earlier, related activities. The children will probably be able to participate in this review by recalling some details on their own.

Adults often make notes of things they must remember. Written outlines, diagrams, and patterns are useful ways of preserving enough of a body of information that the whole can be recreated as necessary. Preschoolers typically do not use such strategies, even when it would be simple to do so and note-taking devices have been supplied. Young children can sometimes be taught to take and use pictorial notes, but the children are frequently so inefficient that their products are useless as memory aids. The age at which children can learn effective note-taking skills depends on the complexity of the task and the nature of the information that must be remembered (Corsini et al., 1968; Rossi & Wittrock, 1971). Teachers might wish to introduce the concept of note taking as part of beginning instruction in reading and writing. For example, in the context of the language-experience method of reading instruction, a teacher can demonstrate how a written record serves as a valuable reminder of past experience.

Memory reflects children's general cognitive capacity in several ways. The more a child understands, the more new information the child can learn and remember with ease. When a child does not seem to be able to remember what has been taught, the difficulty may lie in the child's memory per se, or it may be that the child isn't remembering the material because it doesn't make sense in terms of the child's current level of understanding. During the years between 3 and 8, children are maturing rapidly in their ability to comprehend abstract ideas and logical relationships. How a concept is understood affects how, and how well, it will be remembered.

The development of logical understanding sometimes has very surprising effects on memory. For instance, kindergarteners have been shown a set of sticks arranged in a "staircase" series of decreasing length. When asked to draw the arrangement immediately after they have seen it, the children often made incorrect reproductions. Several months later, with no additional exposure to the arrangement, these children were again asked to draw the sticks. The children often drew better series after this long delay than they had drawn on their first attempt. Children's memory for a single experience changes and may improve over time as they develop more mature understanding of what they *should* have seen (Dahlem, 1969; Finkel & Crowley, 1973; Piaget, 1968).

WHEN DO CHILDREN REMEMBER WELL?

Up to this point, we have emphasized the ways in which the memory of young children differs from that of older children and adults. However, it is just as important to realize that the basic workings of memory are the same at all ages. Thus, procedures that are useful in helping adults or older children to remember may also be useful in helping young children to remember. Indeed, it may be especially important to use these techniques with young children because of the limitations of their memory ability.

Children remember a set of information better if it is familiar and meaningful and if it contains some internal organization (Hall, 1971; Hall & Halperin, 1972; Horowitz et al., 1969; Ross & Youniss, 1969; Rossi & Wittrock, 1971). Since recall is an intelligent process that reflects mental organization, any procedure that helps children to organize new information will also help them to remember. This point has several implications: (1) A series of lessons should have an internal structure. Several lessons planned around a central theme will be remembered better, because the children will be able to relate one day's learning to the next. (2) Lessons should be related to things the children already know from their experience both in and outside of school. (3) Some ideas are difficult to present in any way that makes sense to young children. If a particular lesson seems to be unusually difficult for the children to remember, the teacher might try analyzing the ideas in the lesson and reconsidering the appropriateness of the lesson for that age group (see Chapter 5).

Young children often remember better when they have been actively involved with the material to be remembered. This involvement might consist of naming or otherwise talking or thinking about an experience (Blank & Frank, 1971), or it might consist of touching or manipulating concrete materials (Balling & Myers, 1971; Wolff, 1972; Wolff et al., 1972). One great advantage of real objects as teaching materials is that they encourage all kinds of involvement.

Young children remember material better if they have more than one exposure to it (Brown & Scott, 1971; Hoving et al., 1972; McCarson & Daves, 1972). When children need repetition, they don't find it boring; in fact, much of young children's play can be characterized as the repetition of an achievement over and over until it is thoroughly mastered (Millar, 1968). Repetition does not have to be in the form of a drill in which exactly the same information is presented again and again in the same way. Indeed, children are better able to learn the name of a conceptual category, such as "fruit," if they are given many different examples of items in the category (apples, bananas, peaches, and so on) than if they are given a few examples that are repeated many times (McCarson & Daves, 1972). Children remember pictures better if, weeks after the initial learning, the picture names are used in a story (Hoving et al., 1972).

Young children are likely to remember information that they are interested in and pay attention to. Many of the procedures that facilitate memory may be effective, at least to some degree, because they increase children's attention to the task. Thus the material in Chapter 3 is also directly relevant to a consideration of children's memory and how it might be improved.

Precise age ranges have been omitted from the recommendations in this chapter, in part because of the individual differences in children's memory development, but also because there are great differences in children's performance that depend on the exact nature of the materials and procedures used in a memory task. Procedures such as repetition, active involvement, and labeling, which are vital in helping preschoolers to remember, are also important for older children. Even if children of a certain age can learn or remember "the hard way," they may still benefit from teaching strategies that make memory tasks easier.

Points to Remember

There are a number of strategies teachers might use to help children overcome the limitations of their ability to remember:

1. Young children have excellent ability to recognize perceptual information even after long delays; thus, teachers can use familiar objects, pictures, and sounds to help children remember. Because recognition tasks are easy for preschoolers, they can be used to build confidence and interest.

2. Because young children retain relatively few items of new information, teachers should make sure that each small set of information has been thoroughly learned before presenting additional information. If children have been "overloaded" with new information, a lesson may be impossible to salvage and is best put off to another time.

3. Young children often need repetition in order to learn. A child who has learned a new lesson well enough to give a correct answer once or twice may need considerably more exposure before the memory is secure.

4. Young children remember better when they can get actively involved by talking and thinking about, or working physically with, the materials involved in new experiences.

5. Children remember better when they can give a name to an experience. They may do this spontaneously, but the teacher can help by *making sure* that the children know and use appropriate names, particularly when new experiences or concepts are involved.

6. Information that fits together and makes sense is easier to remember.

7. Teachers should take the limits of young children's short-term memory into account when planning learning tasks. Sometimes a problem can be redesigned so that it has fewer terms or steps. Problems for elementary school children may be easier if they are written down than if they are given orally.

8. Children can be taught to try to remember. Children begin to use memory strategies spontaneously by age 6 or so, but both elementary and preschool children can probably benefit from instruction in strategies such as repeating

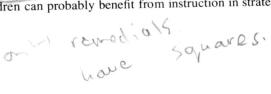
only remedials have squares.

lessons over and over (verbal rehearsal), using physical clues to prompt memory, and "taking notes" in writing or in the form of drawings.

Recommended Reading

Farnham-Diggory, S. (Ed.). *Information processing in children.* New York: Academic Press, 1972.

Piaget, J. *On the development of memory and identity* (E. Duckworth, trans.). Worcester, Mass.: Clark University Press, 1968.

CHAPTER FIVE
LOGICAL THINKING

DIGEST OF RECOMMENDATIONS

1. *Suggested Teaching Technique:* Give young children varied opportunities to exercise their developing understanding of basic logical principles through activities such as the following: (a) putting things into logical groups on the basis of common properties, such as form, color, function, number, or abstract qualities (for example, living versus nonliving), (b) putting things (stacking rings, graduated sticks) into serial order and establishing relationships between two such series (dolls and doll beds of various sizes), and (c) transforming materials and observing how their perceptual properties can be changed back and forth without altering the material's quantity (rolling and squashing clay, bending and straightening wire).

   Rationale: Until age 7 (give or take two years), children's thinking is characterized by an inability to comprehend such general logical principles as classification, seriation, and the conservation of quantity during perceptual transformations. Children's understanding is thought to develop from active manipulation of materials and observation of the changes that occur.

   Selected References: Baldwin, 1967; Bruner, Olver, & Greenfield, 1966; Lloyd, 1971; Lovell, 1971c; Piaget, 1971; Sigel, 1972.

2. *Suggested Teaching Technique:* Try teaching children specific skills, such as counting objects and events or identifying geometric shapes, even if they do not yet understand the system they are using. This teaching should include providing opportunities for children to use manipulable materials to work out problems on their own.

   Rationale: Children attain conservation of number after learning how to count, add, and subtract. Practice in manipulating quantities may help conservation to develop. Programs have been developed that provide a sequence of number-learning activities consistent with the psychological evidence concerning how basic number skills are acquired. Preschool children can learn to identify common Euclidean shapes (for example, circles, triangles, and squares).

   Selected References: Cousins & Abravanel, 1971; Denney, 1972b; Piaget, 1971; Resnick, Wang, & Kaplan, 1973; Winer, 1968; Wohlwill, 1960.

3. When teaching computational or measurement skills to young elementary school children, give them practice in all types of situations in which they will be expected to use the skill (for example, measuring with different units, averaging numbers of different magnitudes).

   Rationale: Young children tend to learn these skills in terms of specific instances, and learning is not likely to generalize spontaneously to new situations.

   Selected References: Lovell, 1971a, 1971b, 1971c.

4. *Suggested Teaching Technique:* Give children opportunities to analyze space in terms of its topological properties (for example, holes and boundaries).

   Rationale: Young children seem to be naturally attentive to topological properties of space. Understanding of topological properties may be the only kind of spatial understanding that preschool children can handle well.

   Selected References: Laurendeau & Pinard, 1970; Piaget & Inhelder, 1956; Sauvy & Sauvy, 1974.

5. *Suggested Teaching Technique:* Give young children extensive practice in discriminating and using projective space relationships, especially left and right.

   Rationale: Young children's understanding of space and spatial relationships is limited by their logical immaturity. Projective spatial relations and measurement are particularly difficult. Left/right distinctions are more difficult than front/back and up/down distinctions. Children learn to coordinate spatial relations among objects years after they learn spatial features of single objects. Practice helps children to learn spatial distinctions.

   Selected References: Asso & Wyke, 1971; Elkind, 1961; Goodnow, 1972; Harris, 1972; Strayer & Ames, 1972.

6. *Suggested Teaching Technique:* Give young children practice in predicting how spatial arrangements might look from different viewpoints.

   Rationale: This skill typically develops during the early elementary school years without formal teaching. Young children act as if they know that the view from different locations must vary, but they can't predict just *how* it varies.

   Selected References: Fishbein, Lewis, & Kuffer, 1972; Laurendeau & Pinard, 1970; Selman, 1971; Shantz & Watson, 1971.

7. *Suggested Teaching Technique:* Supplement teaching of computational formulas for measurement (for example, area = length x width) with experiences that demonstrate the concrete logic of the process (for example, adding small units of standard area).

   Rationale: Children who have learned the standard formulas and techniques of measurement may not understand the underlying logic or be able to generalize their skills to new units or situations. A certain degree of intellectual maturity is necessary for children to understand the general principles involved in measuring area or volume.

Selected References: Lovell, 1971b, 1971c.

HOW DOES CHILDREN'S THINKING CHANGE BETWEEN AGE 3 AND AGE 8?

This chapter introduces important principles of Swiss philosopher-psychologist Jean Piaget's theory of the development of children's thinking. A general discussion of the theory and its relevance to the classroom is followed by a discussion of its application to two content areas: how children learn to understand numbers and how they learn to understand space. These content areas have been chosen to illustrate how changes with age in children's general patterns of thinking affect their ability to learn specific skills.

Piaget's theory is based on his view that older children do not simply *know* more than younger children but *think* in qualitatively different ways. The rate at which thinking skills develop varies among children and among cultures, but all children, according to Piaget, go through the same sequence of stages.

Piaget categorizes preschool-age children as "preoperational"—that is, prelogical. Their thinking is dominated by perceptual processes, by what *seems* to be rather than by what logically *must be*. Preoperational children have not mastered the systems of logical operations that characterize the thinking of older children.   *t a i l   on   gerbil.*

The shift from preoperational to operational, or logical, thinking is a gradual process that begins, roughly, at about age 5 or 6 and continues until about age 9. Throughout this period and beyond, children gain the ability to apply their logic systems to an ever-increasing range of situations (Baldwin, 1967; Piaget, 1968, 1971; Piaget & Inhelder, 1956). The transition from preoperational to operational thinking can be described in terms of the mastery of three types of logical problems: classification, seriation, and conservation.

Classification. Classification involves grouping events in terms of their similarities (within classes) and differences (between classes). The child who takes a pile of red and blue blocks and sorts them into one pile of red and one pile of blue is classifying the blocks. Similarly, the child who mentally associates flowers with trees as members of the superordinate class "plants" is performing a classification operation.

Preschool children can often form reasonably consistent groups of objects or concepts if they can work from a single common attribute (that is, form *or* color *or* function). They tend to be unable to classify things in more than one way at a time. Rarely will they produce, or give evidence of having conceptualized, classification hierarchies such as the one diagrammed in Figure 1.

Practice in considering how objects and ideas are similar and different from one another can, however, improve young children's classification performance (Denney, 1972b; Fowler, 1965; Sigel, 1972).

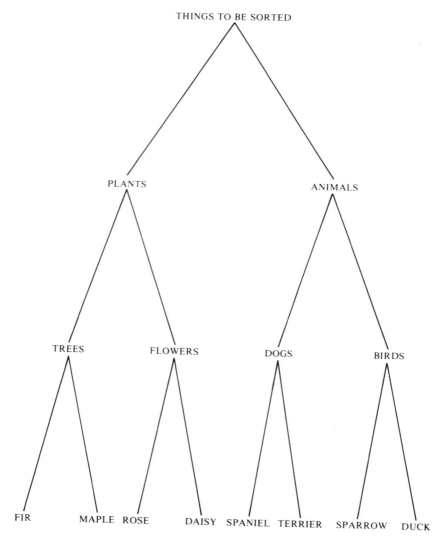

Figure 1. A hierarchical classification system.

Teachers who want to evaluate the extent to which their children have mastered the operation of classification should be aware that success in classification tasks tends to vary with the number and nature of the materials or ideas to be sorted out, the dimensions defining possible classification arrangements, and the instructions given (Brown & Campione, 1971; Cazden, 1972; Denney, 1972b; Katz, 1971; Sigel, 1972; White, 1971). Like most cognitive advances, classification skills emerge gradually in a limited range of situations, broadening and deepening with further experience.

Demonstration of the ability to group objects in multiple, hierarchical classes is one of several signs that a child has developed a working understanding of the logic of classification. Age estimates vary by several years, but full competence in a classification task like the one presented in Figure 1 may not come until a child is 7 or 8 years old. Between the ages of 5 and 7, children are prone to inconsistencies such as erratic shifting in mid-task from one basis of classification to another. For example, a 6-year-old might begin to separate the items in Figure 1 into separate groups of plants and animals, then move the sparrow over to the tree group because "birds live in trees."

When children have developed some implicit understanding of the logic of classification, they are ready to grasp a variety of logical and mathematical concepts. For instance, understanding the classification hierarchy of Figure 1 requires appreciation of the principle of *class inclusion* and the concept of *reversibility*, ideas that are also central to an understanding of the number system and of the process of addition and subtraction.

In Figure 1, the class *animals* includes, or equals the sum of, its component subclasses *dogs* and *birds*. The inclusive class "animals" is created by adding the dogs to the birds. Conversely, if the dogs are removed from the set of animals, only the birds remain. The processes of combining classes and separating them reverse, or cancel out, each other.

Similarly the number system can be conceptualized as quantities (classes or sets) that include other quantities (classes or sets). Just as the class of animals in Figure 1 includes birds and dogs, the quantity 10 includes the quantities 8 and 2. Expressed in another way, any set of 10 things includes a set of 8 things and a set of 2 things. Like the operations of combining and separating classes, addition and subtraction are opposite procedures that reverse each other. The addition of 2 things and 8 things to yield 10 things is reversed by the subtraction of 2 things from 10 things to yield 8 things.

In a traditional mathematics program, a kindergartener may spend several weeks memorizing addition facts and then move on to several weeks of concentration on subtraction facts. Such a child is likely to be quite unaware of the connection between the knowledge that $8 + 2 = 10$ and the knowledge that $10 - 8 = 2$. Without such insight, learning may be slow, incomplete, and unstable.

The understanding of class inclusion and reversibility has implications for many areas besides mathematics learning. For example, many preschoolers have difficulty grasping the idea that a state includes many cities and is itself included in a larger unit, the nation. Thus they may deny that a person who lives in Seattle (is a member of the class *Seattle residents*) also lives in Washington State (is a member of the inclusive class *Washington residents*). Mature thinking and language are pervasively influenced by principles that children are just beginning to comprehend in the years from 3 through 8.

Seriation.   Mastery of the operation of seriation—that is, the ability to order events in terms of differences on a single dimension—is another basic intellectual skill that distinguishes preoperational from operational children. Even before age 3, children can order objects in terms of perceptual properties such as size. They are delighted with seriation toys—stacking rings and nested boxes, for instance—and easily put the components in order after an initial period of trial and error (Lovell, 1971b, 1971c). Older children's logical understanding of seriation (as opposed to preschoolers' perceptual understanding) involves mastery of the logical operation of *transitivity*. As applied to the relation *larger than*, transitivity is the principle that, if A is larger than B and B is larger than C, then A *must be* larger than C. Understanding transitivity makes it possible for children to put a collection of things in order without directly comparing each of the items with every other one.

Estimates of the age at which children master transitivity and seriation differ, depending on the task used to measure the ability and the type of response (correct performance or correct explanation) required to "pass" the test. Some estimates indicate mastery of transitivity at age 5 or 6, others at 7 or 8 (Brainerd, 1973b; Lovell, 1971a; Trabasso, 1973). Although several different tasks have been used to assess children's seriation ability, all of the tasks involve materials and procedures that make it difficult for children to be successful if they use only perceptual cues.

Many logical and mathematical problems are based on the principle of seriation. The number system, for instance, can be described in terms of seriation as well as in terms of class inclusion (Brainerd, 1973a; Copeland, 1974; Lovell, 1971a, 1971c; Resnick, Wang, & Kaplan, 1973). If numerals are thought of as an ordered progression on a number line, relations among them can be described in terms of serial properties.

Children who have mastered seriation should have no difficulty in establishing the correspondence between the progression of sets of increasing quantities and the numeral names for these sets. With this understanding, children logically conclude that, if 4 is more than 3 and 5 is more than 4, then 5 *must be* more than 3. Furthermore, children who have mastered the reversibility of serial relations can also conclude that 3 *must be* less than 5. Children who do not fully understand seriation might answer such questions correctly with small, familiar numerals that represent easily countable quantities, but they are likely to be stumped in more challenging situations:

> *Adult:* Which is more, 29 or 30?
> *Child:* 30.
> *Adult:* Which is more, 30 or 33?
> *Child:* 33.
> *Adult:* Which is more, 33 or 29?
> *Child:* I want to go home now.

Conservation.   The principle of conservation of quantity is basic to adult logic. It is obvious to adults that the number of buttons in a row is unchanged if the buttons are spread far apart or bunched together, that a bent wire has the same length as it had when it was straight, that the distance between two tables is not changed if a chair is placed in the intervening space, or that the quantity of liquid in a tall, narrow glass is not altered when the liquid is poured into a short, wide glass. This invariance of quantity despite such perceptual changes is not, however, apparent to young children. Preoperational children do not realize that perceptual changes in one dimension (height of liquid in a glass, the space between buttons) are compensated for by changes in other dimensions (the circumference of the liquid, the total space covered by the buttons) or that the changes are reversible (the liquid can be poured back; nothing has been added or taken away). Since young children's judgments of quantity are perceptual rather than logical, they do not have concepts of quantity independent of misleading perceptual cues. Thus they are likely to judge that manipulations such as those illustrated in Figure 2 *change* a quantity. A widely spaced array of objects is said to contain more objects than a dense array; a tall, thin glass is said to contain more liquid than a short, fat glass.

Preschoolers, for instance, are not readily convinced that one large cookie is as desirable as two small ones or that the juice in a short, wide glass is really as fair a share as the juice in another child's taller but narrower glass. Preschool children seem to "center" their attention in such cases on a particularly compelling aspect of the perceptual situation, such as the height of the juice in a glass (Curcio, Kattef, Levine, & Robbins, 1972; O'Bryan & Boersma, 1971; Piaget, 1968; Pufall & Shaw, 1972). Explanations from the teacher are unlikely to change the child's judgment.

Starting at about age 5, and continuing through the elementary school years, children gradually acquire conservation of various quantity concepts. The idea of number is usually mastered first, followed by length and distance. The conservation of mass, liquid quantity, weight, and volume come later; many 8-year-olds, for instance, might fail the conservation-of-liquid task illustrated in Figure 2 (Brainerd & Brainerd, 1972; Elkind, 1961; Elkind & Schoenfeld, 1972; Moynahan & Glick, 1972).

CONSERVATION OF NUMBER

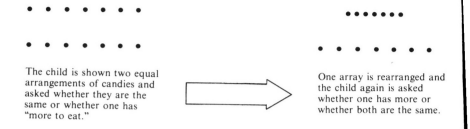

The child is shown two equal arrangements of candies and asked whether they are the same or whether one has "more to eat."

One array is rearranged and the child again is asked whether one has more or whether both are the same.

CONSERVATION OF LIQUID

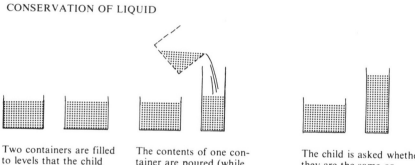

Two containers are filled to levels that the child agrees represent equal amounts.

The contents of one container are poured (while the child watches) into a container of a different shape.

The child is asked whether they are the same or whether one has "more to drink."

Figure 2. Examples of tests for conservation of number and conservation of liquid quantity.

Like classification ability, conservation emerges gradually. Children often make correct conservation judgments before they are able to explain their decisions. Small differences in the way conservation tasks are administered, such as eliminating the requirement for a verbal explanation or reducing the number of objects in a number-conservation task, can affect how well children will perform (Gelman, 1972; Papalia & Hooper, 1971; Wohlwill & Lowe, 1972). Children who are at the transitional stage for a particular type of conservation are also likely to make "conserving" *predictions* about the perceptual effect that will result from an action such as pouring a liquid into a narrower glass but fall back to a nonconserving judgment when confronted by the misleading results of that operation (Brainerd & Brainerd, 1972; Curcio et al., 1972; Larsen & Flavell, 1970; Piaget, 1968).

Conservation, like classification and seriation, is a basic logical operation that children must master before they can fully understand a number of the logical and mathematical concepts taught in the early school years. Until children understand conservation of number, for instance, they cannot really comprehend the meaning of the number 3, much less the meaning of $2 + 3 = 5$. Similarly, conservation of length is prerequisite for understanding measurement. Nonconserving children may be able to do these tasks after a fashion, but they do not understand what they are doing in the way an older child or an adult would. To measure the circumference of a finger, for instance, an adult might hold a string firmly around the finger, mark the string, then straighten it against a ruler to determine its length and, therefore, the circumference of the finger. Young children who do not understand that the length of the string is the same whether the string is in a circle or lying straight have difficulty in accepting the validity of this technique.

Children who have not yet mastered conservation can still benefit from practice in activities such as counting, computing, and measuring, but they will not fully understand these operations until they begin to conserve. Conservation of number follows the acquisition of basic computational skill (Gruen, 1965; Winer, 1968; Wohlwill, 1960; Wohlwill & Lowe, 1972). Practice in learning the correspondence between quantities and numerals probably also helps children to reach an understanding of conservation; that understanding can then open a new perspective on the computation process.

When confronted with evidence that young children think differently from older children, the teacher's natural desire is to find a way of teaching young children to think "better." There is, in fact, evidence that young children *can* be taught to classify, to seriate, and to conserve at levels considerably beyond what would be expected of their age group (Fowler, 1965; Gelman, 1969; Sigel, 1972).

The greatest amount of research effort has been devoted to developing techniques for teaching young children to make mature judgments in the various conservation problems. A number of the training procedures thus developed have significantly changed children's judgments on the specific problem used for training and, in some cases, have also increased the likelihood of children's making conservation judgments on other types of problems (Gelman, 1969, 1972; Peters, 1970; Siegler & Liebert, 1972). In general, children do not learn conservation responses by listening to lectures (Gruen, 1965; Rosenthal & Zimmerman, 1972), but they do learn to make conservation judgments through experiences such as working with materials that focus attention on the relationships to be learned (Gelman, 1969), debating with small groups of classmates who already understand the principle

(Murray, 1972), or by watching their peers give mature responses to a conservation problem (Botvin & Murray, 1975). However, initially nonconserving children who have been trained to make conservation judgments do not always explain their judgments in the same way as "natural" conservers do (Botvin & Murray, 1975).

Despite evidence that children can, with intensive training, be taught to demonstrate more mature logic, teachers who are considering trying such specific training in their own classrooms might first consider several basic points derived from Piaget's theory and from experimental studies of children's thinking.

1. Children's thinking matures without formal teaching. Even children who have never been to school eventually develop operational thinking. The experiences critical for its development are therefore available in children's normal daily activities. The *rate* of development may vary with the kinds of experience and "push" offered by the child's environment (Bruner, Olver, & Greenfield, 1966; Ginsburg, 1972; Lloyd, 1971; Lovell, 1971c); however, a school curriculum designed to foster the development of operational thinking will not necessarily have any greater effect on the development of young children's reasoning than will any other good curriculum (Bingham-Newman, Saunders, & Hooper, 1974).

2. Children learn best when they are ready to learn. Children whose minds have developed to the point of generating new ways of thinking make the transition easily, while children who are not ready may learn only after prolonged effort (Ginsburg, 1972).

3. Teaching children to solve one type of logical problem does not result in a general leap in cognitive maturity. Teaching classification, for instance, helps children to classify, but it doesn't accelerate the development of conservation, seriation, or English grammar (Almy, 1971; Bingham-Newman et al., 1974).

4. Although individual children differ in the rate of their progress through the developmental stages involved in acquiring logical skills, they also differ in the breadth and flexibility of their understanding at each stage. It may be more important for teachers to stress activities that promote thorough, diversified mastery of reasoning at or only *slightly* beyond the child's existing level than to push toward a new level (Lovell, 1971c).

Activities involving classification, seriation, or conservation do have a place in the preschool or early elementary school classroom. As children play at putting things into groups or series or at pounding masses of clay into various shapes, they gain invaluable experience that facilitates the gradual maturation of their thinking. There is an important difference, however, between giving children opportunities to expand their thinking and attempting to make children think in the way that adults do. Piaget's point is missed by a teacher who sorts objects into an adult classification system and then tries to communicate the logic of that system to a group of young children. Children can be drilled into parroting that all small, blue things should go together or that two glasses hold the same amount of water, but this kind of activity probably has little long-term value. Standard tests of logical understanding can be helpful when used as diagnostic aids for assessing children's level of understanding. However, such tests should not be used to teach children the circumscribed patterns of responses defined by the tests (Almy, 1971; Evans, 1975).

HOW DO CHILDREN DEVELOP AN UNDERSTANDING OF NUMBERS?

The research just discussed has shown that most preschool children do not have a well-developed concept of number. To truly comprehend numbers, children need a certain degree of general intellectual maturity. Very young children can, however, acquire a variety of basic skills in dealing with quantity and number. These skills are useful in themselves and may facilitate the long-term development of more complete understanding.

The two number skills most often taught preschoolers are counting and learning number names. These apparently simple tasks actually present quite a challenge to the young child. For instance, a 3-year-old who is beginning to learn to count might be able to correctly give the number of objects in any set containing up to five items but falter when asked to count six or seven things. The child seems to be unsure of which numerals follow 5, while using the sequence up to 5 without hesitation.

Many young children can recite names of numbers in serial order without being able to use these names to count objects. The ability to recite a string of numbers is only one step in learning to count. Children must also acquire the ability to pair each numeral with the "marking-off" of an object. When 2- or 3-year-olds "count," they often chant a series of number names in one tempo and point to the objects counted in a completely different tempo, so that the recital of several number names might correspond to the touching of only one object, or vice versa.

Counting is easiest when each object can be physically set aside as it is counted. Under these conditions a child has less trouble determining which items have already been counted and which remain; errors of repetition or omission are therefore less likely (Resnick, Wang & Kaplan, 1973; Sinclair, 1970). Counting is somewhat more difficult if each object cannot be moved as it is counted. In this case, a child must pick a starting point, create a systematic order in which the objects are to be counted, and carry out the counting procedure. Children seem to handle this problem by first grouping the objects into a visually ordered arrangement and then proceeding to count (Resnick et al, 1973).

While learning to count, preschoolers can simultaneously be acquiring the ability to recognize and use written number symbols that will be needed when arithmetic problems shift from actual sets of objects to symbolic representations of those sets. Figure 3 outlines possible training sequences for counting and learning to use numerals. These sequences were derived from Piaget's theory and from research on the natural order in which children acquire counting skills.

The training program from which sample units are presented in Figure 3 suggests teaching numbers up to 5 before attempting to work with large numbers. This suggestion is based on the research findings that children normally acquire a range of skills (counting, adding, and subtracting) with numbers up to 5 before beginning to master the same set of skills with larger numbers (Wang, Resnick, & Boozer, 1971). Thus, once children master the counting and one-to-one correspondence sequences illustrated for numbers to 5, they go through a similar sequence of activities involving numbers from 6 to 10.

Preschool children who have learned to count still have a great deal to learn about numbers. They have not yet acquired a *concept* of number—an understanding of the basic properties of the number system. The limits of preschoolers' comprehension are apparent when they are asked to do something unexpected, such as starting to count from 3 onward or saying what number comes *before* 5 (Kersh, 1974).

The number system can be viewed in two ways. In one view, the system is characterized as an ordered progression, a series in which each number has a fixed position relative to the other members. Thus, 3 is the number that comes before (is less than) 4 and comes after (is greater than) 2. Children's developing understanding of the *ordinal* aspect of the number system is closely tied to their understanding of the general concept of seriation (Brainerd, 1973a).

The number system can also be viewed as a system that defines the "manyness," or *cardinality*, of a set. Thus, any two sets of three elements are the same in cardinal number even if one set contains three apples and the other, three oranges. The cardinal number 3 is what all possible sets of three things have in common (Brainerd, 1973a).

Learning to understand cardinal number (two things, three things) and ordinal number (second place, third place) is no easy task, since both concepts have to be mastered in their own right and in relation to one

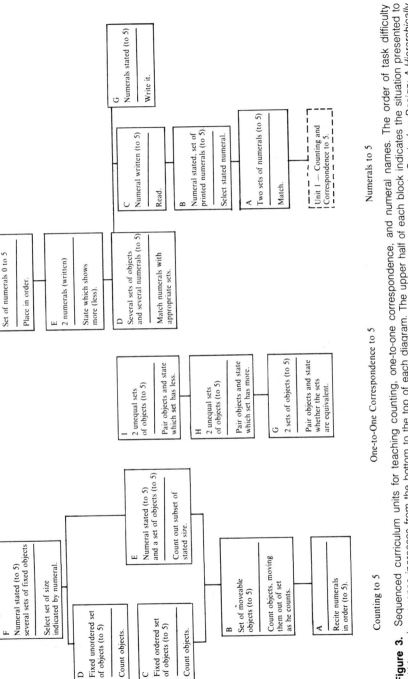

Figure 3. Sequenced curriculum units for teaching counting, one-to-one correspondence, and numeral names. The order of task difficulty within each sequence increases from the bottom to the top of each diagram. The upper half of each block indicates the situation presented to the child, while the lower half describes what the child is expected to do. (Adapted from *Behavior Analysis in Curriculum Design: A Hierarchically Sequenced Introductory Mathematics Curriculum*, by L. B. Resnick, M. C. Wang, and J. Kaplan. Monograph 2, 1970, University of Pittsburgh Learning Research and Development Center. Reprinted by permission.)

Counting to 5

One-to-One Correspondence to 5

Numerals to 5

F
Numeral stated (to 5)
several sets of fixed objects
———
Select set of size
indicated by numeral.

D
Fixed unordered set
of objects (to 5)
———
Count objects.

C
Fixed ordered set
of objects (to 5)
———
Count objects.

E
Numeral stated (to 5)
and a set of objects (to 5)
———
Count out subset of
stated size.

B
Set of moveable
objects (to 5)
———
Count objects, moving
them out of set
as he counts.

A
Recite numerals
in order (to 5).

I
2 unequal sets
of objects (to 5)
———
Pair objects and state
which set has less.

H
2 unequal sets
of objects (to 5)
———
Pair objects and state
which set has more.

G
2 sets of objects (to 5)
———
Pair objects and state
whether the sets
are equivalent.

Set of numerals 0 to 5
———
Place in order.

E
2 numerals (written)
———
State which shows
more (less).

D
Several sets of objects
and several numerals (to 5)
———
Match numerals with
appropriate sets.

G
Numerals stated (to 5)
———
Write it.

C
Numeral written (to 5)
———
Read.

B
Numeral stated, set of
printed numerals (to 5)
———
Select stated numeral.

A
Two sets of numerals (to 5)
———
Match.

Unit I — Counting and
Correspondence to 5.

another. Many of the "new-math" curricula suggest a variety of learning activities designed to help young children master the basic concepts underlying the number system (Copeland, 1974; Lovell, 1971a, 1971c).

Children's development of an understanding of the number system is slow to reach completion. In general, children seem to learn a particular skill, such as counting or addition, some time before they acquire a conceptual understanding of the operations associated with that skill. For instance, the preschool child who can count with great facility has not yet achieved conservation of number and will not be at all distressed by the contradiction of counting two sets of objects, reaching the same total for each set, and yet judging that one set contains more when it is spread out so that it covers more space (Sinclair, 1970). Many of the general principles of the number system, such as the idea of averaging or the effects of combining odd and even numbers, seem to be gradually mastered between the ages of 8 and 11. Before age 8, children are likely to master an operation in a specific instance without seeing the generality of the rule (Lovell, 1971a). Teachers should not assume, therefore, that young children who appear to understand an operation in a given instance are being perverse if they fail to apply the operation in a new instance.

One major contribution of psychological research to mathematics teaching has been the demonstration that young children learn mathematics most readily through extensive experience with the manipulation of real objects, forms, and pictures (see, for example, Lovell, 1971c). Symbols such as written numerals or addition and subtraction signs become meaningful after children have acquired a conceptual, logical understanding of the operations signified by the written notation (Piaget, 1971). For example, a group of primary-grade children learning the concept of place value may have great fun, and an effective learning experience, by making trades of pennies for dimes. A slightly more advanced activity might involve trading play-money bills in one-, ten-, and hundred-dollar denominations. The transition from trading games to use of the written place-value notation can be facilitated by an intermediate activity in which the children are asked to keep a written record of their financial transactions (Cook, 1976).

Individual children differ considerably in their need to rely on concrete experience as an aid to reasoning. One approach to working with children whose learning styles differ is to introduce each new concept in the context of an opportunity to manipulate concrete materials. Some children will move quickly from the necessarily slow-paced manipulation of blocks, rods, or play money to more efficient mental or paper-and-pencil calculation. Other children will need more extended experience with the perceptual aids (Cook, 1976).

HOW DO YOUNG CHILDREN DEVELOP AN UNDERSTANDING OF SPACE AND SPATIAL RELATIONSHIPS?

When children are asked to read "from left to right," to measure the daily growth of the classroom bean crop, or to trace on a map the route from home to school, they are being asked to use some sort of spatial information or spatial reasoning ability. Some types of spatial problems are easy for young children, but others are quite difficult. It's easier to predict which tasks will be easy and which difficult if spatial problems are divided into three general categories: problems concerned with the *topological* properties of space, problems concerned with *projective relationships*, and problems concerned with *measurement*.

When space is considered in terms of the system known in formal mathematics as *topology*, the only relevant properties are those that do not change if the space is stretched or distorted (Baldwin, 1967). For this "rubber-sheet" geometry, there is no distinction between a large circle and a small circle, for the dimension of size is irrelevant. Furthermore, a circle is no different from a square, for there is no distinction between straight and curved lines. The properties that are significant in the topological system are such features as continuity, neighboringness, and betweenness. For example, a "C" and a "U" are topologically similar, because both forms consist of a broken line that partially encloses a space. The "C" and "U" forms are both topologically different from an "O," which fully encloses an area. Because the topological system relies on distinctions that young children have a natural propensity to notice, such as open versus closed, it is a relatively easy system for preschoolers and early elementary school children to work with.

In contrast, learning the system of *projective* space seems to be one of the most difficult tasks of the early years. This system involves relationships of distance and direction. Children must learn to coordinate their own egocentric (self-centered) points of view with other systems of reference. They must also learn a complex verbal system to label their understanding of these relationships. The difficulties are such that children's ability to use the projective system is not fully adequate until age 6, 7, or even later.

Interdependent with the projective system is the *Euclidean* system of analyzing space. This system emphasizes distinctions such as the differences between lines and curves and quantitative features such as numbers of angles and lengths of sides. The Euclidean system is familiar to most adults, since it is the basis for the measurement and computation skills traditionally taught in school—the definition of a parallelogram, for instance, or the formula for computing the circumference of a circle. Young children pick up the basic features of this system in preschool or early school experiences. They can learn to distinguish and to label such forms as triangles, squares, circles, and hexagons. It is not until well into the elementary school years, however, that they understand more advanced Euclidean problems, such as the measurement of space and distance.

The development of children's understanding of topological, projective, and Euclidean space is described in more detail in the following pages.

Topology.   There is evidence that preschool children are very sensitive to certain topological properties. In some circumstances, young children act as if they are coping with topological "laws" but not with the laws of the projective and Euclidean systems. Consider the performance of children asked to place a row of miniature lampposts so that they make a straight line between two miniature houses. Preschool children (up to about age 5) have great difficulty in making a straight line of lamps spaced evenly between the houses. For example, if the houses are placed at opposite corners of a rectangular surface, preschool children are not likely to set up the lampposts in a straight diagonal. Their attempts to connect the houses will tend to reflect a "pull" to the "neighborhood" (a topological feature) of the surface on which they are working. The lampposts will be placed not in a straight line, but in a curve following first the base and then the side of the surface (Laurendeau & Pinard, 1970).

Another task used to test children's sensitivity to topological properties requires the child to recognize or match shapes varying in either topological or Euclidean features. Children's judgments indicate attention to topological features, such as the presence or absence of holes, as well as to certain Euclidean properties, such as whether an edge is straight or curved. Preschoolers make correct matching judgments on Euclidean properties if the shapes used are familiar ones, such as circles and squares (Cousins & Abravanel, 1971; Dodwell, 1963; Laurendeau & Pinard, 1970). When the shapes are less familiar, children are more likely to match them according to their topological properties. If a child is attending to "holes," for instance, an elliptical "doughnut" will be matched with a straight-edged, rectangular doughnut rather than with a plain ellipse.

Children's ability to utilize projective and Euclidean features of spatial problems varies with the exact nature of the task and perhaps with their educational experience (Cousins & Abravanel, 1971; Dodwell, 1971). However, it does seem that young children can deal well with concepts such as continuity, boundaries, and holes. How closely this competence resembles topology as a formal system constructed by mathematicians is unknown, nor is it important psychologically. What matters to the teacher is that consideration of topological properties provides a realm of activities in which very young children can stretch their minds and have encouraging, successful experience in handling spatial problems. Topological principles can be used as the basis for an endless variety of games and puzzles for both preschool and elementary school children (see, for example, Sauvy & Sauvy, 1974). Preschoolers, for instance, can study the nature of holes during sand or water play with funnels, cups, and sieves. The teacher might help the children to discover which objects permit the sand or water to flow through and which do not. Older children can explore the idea of continuity by creating and solving paper-and-pencil mazes.

Projective space. Both formal research and informal observation confirm the theoretical argument (Piaget & Inhelder, 1956) that the system of projective spatial relationships is a major challenge to a young child. Even though 3-year-olds are quite capable of indicating that a picture of an upside-down house is "wrong," they do not regard orientation as a significant cue when asked whether two pictures show the "same thing" (McGurk, 1972). Since the identity of any real object is indeed constant despite its apparent orientation, children's tendency to ignore orientation is quite reasonable.

Children's ability to use orientation in their drawing or writing is even weaker than their ability to attend to orientation when making a discrimination (Asso & Wyke, 1971; Strayer & Ames, 1972). A 6-year-old who never reads from right to left and who usually writes correctly may occasionally lapse and produce constructions such as "yaJ oT" in addressing a note to a friend. There is evidence that giving children specific training in using orientation cues to make a discrimination will produce improvement in their writing as well (Strayer & Ames, 1972).

One source of difficulty in young children's writing may be their tendency to write in accordance with a few set habits or "rules." More often than not, they try to start at the top of a form, move from left to right, and use a continuous stroke. Persistence in such habits can lead a child who should "know better" into production of forms such as "И" for "N" (Goodnow, 1972).

Of all the concepts associated with object orientation and with the relations among objects, left and right cause young children the greatest difficulty. The left/right distinction is harder than front/back or up/down distinctions (Harris, 1972). By second grade, children have excellent command of up/down and front/back but still are confused about left/right when asked such questions as "Is the pencil to the left or to the right of the matches?" Perhaps left and right are more difficult because nature has not provided human beings with a natural perceptual reference system for learning these concepts. Gravity provides us with a natural "down" and the structure of our bodies and visual orientation helps to clarify the front/back distinction, but left and right are learned without such perceptual help (H. H. Clark, 1973).

Children first master left and right in relation to parts of their own bodies. Most 5- or 6-year-olds can make these identifications correctly (Elkind, 1961; Harris, 1972). Identifying the left and right body parts of another person is much more difficult, particularly if the person is sitting face-to-face with the child, and this skill is not secure until age 7 or 8 (Elkind, 1961). More difficult still is the coordination of positional relations among a set of objects. According to Piaget, children first learn left and right as properties of particular objects, starting with their own bodies, and later come to understand the system of left and right *relations* among objects. To understand this system fully, children not only must be able to determine, say, that the pencil is "to the left of the matches" but must be aware that the pencil (in the middle of the set of objects) is also "to the right of the keys" (Harris, 1972).

Because an understanding of projective-space concepts is so important to the basic skills of reading and writing, and because this understanding is normally slow to develop, teachers should make a special effort to provide opportunities for learning and relearning the use of these concepts. Furthermore, since children's first grasp of projective-space concepts will be limited to specific contexts, teachers should emphasize a large number of possible contexts. In particular, children who have mastered "left side" and "right side" as properties of particular objects may still need practice in left and right as relative positions.

Children's difficulties in understanding projective space are particularly apparent when they are asked to judge how a spatial arrangement would differ when seen from different points of view. One task frequently used to assess children's ability to coordinate visual perspectives involves a miniature landscape with mountains or other large obstructions that can block off objects, such as miniature animals, from the view of a doll placed at a particular point on the tableau. Young children are rarely able to give an accurate assessment of what the doll "sees" and may respond as if the doll's perspective were the same as their own. The argument has been made that young children's performance on such tasks reflects their egocentric thinking (Laurendeau & Pinard, 1970; Piaget & Inhelder, 1956).

Recent evidence indicates, however, that children as young as 3 or 4 can sometimes make perspective predictions correctly if the task is simple enough. For instance, 3-year-olds are able to rotate a turntable holding several animals to the correct position when an adult, standing in turn at various positions around the table, asks "show me the side of the mouse" (Shantz &

Watson, 1971). Furthermore, the errors that young children make on perspective tasks are not always egocentric errors. Overall errors decrease as children get older, but specifically egocentric errors do not invariably decrease and may sometimes increase, perhaps as a transitional stage preceding full mastery of the task (Fishbein, Lewis, & Kuffer, 1972).

Since the extent and nature of children's errors vary with the specific nature of the perspective task, it seems reasonable to propose that young children are often aware that things look different from different points of view—that their own perspective is not the only one possible. However, when the tasks are complicated, children have difficulty in imagining or expressing what the proper point of view should be and may suggest their own viewpoint, knowing it is wrong, in their desire to provide some reasonable answer (Fishbein et al., 1972; Laurendeau & Pinard, 1970; Selman, 1971; Shantz & Watson, 1971).

Children's performances on perspective tasks show patterns similar to their performances on another purported test of egocentrism, the "blind listener" communication task discussed in Chapter 2. In both cases children seem to know that their own perspective or knowledge is not universal, that others may see things differently or need different information. In both cases, young children perform much better when the task is extremely simple. In communication tasks, training procedures that show children what the needs of the listener are and how they can tailor their speaking to those needs have led to improved performance. Similar strategies might be effective in helping children to become aware of how things look from different perspectives. For example, a teacher might create situations in which children must describe a visual display from the viewpoint of another child sitting opposite or at right angles to the speaker. The children can compare what they see, and the teacher can help them to analyze and predict the view from different perspectives.

Measurement. Another great challenge for young children is understanding the quantitative measurement of space and distance. Measurement, as a rote skill, is fairly easy for young children to learn. If all that they are required to do is to line up the end of a ruler with the end of an object and read off the ruler mark corresponding to the other end of the object, 5- or 6-year-olds can often succeed. Psychological research indicates, however, that children this young will probably not have mastered the concepts underlying the measurement process: if the task is changed slightly so that they cannot rely on rote-learned skill, their competence falters. True understanding of measurement requires, according to Piaget's theory, the ability to use several logical operations (Lovell, 1971b, 1971c).

In essence, measurement of distance or space depends on the division of the length or area into standard units. These arbitrary standard units (such as inches, centimeters, square feet, or acres) can then be summed to give the total expanse of the space in question. Thus, one logical operation that children must master is *class inclusion*—the addition of several parts to form a whole.

An understanding of *transitivity* and *seriation* is also essential to the use of standard units of measure and to any comparison of length, size, weight, and so forth. If one melon weighs less than a pound and another weighs more than a pound, we know that the second melon must be heavier than the first even if we don't have a balance available to compare their weights directly.

Measurement also depends on the attainment of *conservation*. Meaningful measurement of length is not possible if, for instance, children don't yet understand that the length of a stretched-out paper clip is the same as its length when it is coiled. Similarly, children's attempts to measure distance are likely to be affected by their inability to understand that the distance between two objects is not changed by placing additional objects between the first two (Lovell, 1971b, 1971c).

Thus, Piagetian theory stresses that comprehension of measurement requires an understanding of the class-inclusion principle, of seriation and transitivity, and of conservation of number, length, and distance. This understanding is thought not to emerge until the elementary school years, beginning at about age 6 or 7. Children would therefore not be expected to understand measurement until age 7 or later—perhaps much later. There is some evidence to support this prediction.

In one study, a few children showed mastery of length measurement at age 6, but the majority did not succeed until age 8 or later. The measurement task required the children to judge which of a pair of multi-angled lines was longer, using a 2-inch piece of cardboard as a standard unit of length (Larsen & Flavell, 1970).

The results of another study of measurement (Lovell, 1971b) indicate that some children who appear to know how to measure don't actually understand what they're doing. According to their teachers, the 8- to 10-year-old children in this study had all learned to measure area by the usual procedure of multiplying length by width. The children were given eight right triangles that they were to use to *compare* the areas of an 8-inch by 8-inch square and a 4-inch by 16-inch rectangle. The task was a hard one, since all of the triangles together could cover only half of the total area of each figure. Children who started out using the triangle units appropriately were often stumped when they ran out of triangles. No child below age 8 and only half of the 8-year-olds discovered the correct procedure of using the triangle tiles to block off as much as possible, noting the boundary of the area covered, then reusing the tiles to measure the area remaining. Furthermore, many children who were able to compare two areas by using this technique were still not able to master a similar problem, which involved using a small card as a unit of measure to calculate the area of a figure.

These children had learned to compute areas in inches but did not understand that areas could also be expressed in other units, such as "blue cards." Lovell (1971b, 1971c) suggests that teachers supplement instruction in the length-by-width method of area computation with experience in measuring area by adding units of standard area.

Points to Remember

An awareness of children's competencies and of how they develop enables teachers to schedule each learning experience at the point in development when children are most likely to profit from the experience. Such awareness also provides teachers with a sense of what problems and misunderstandings might be expected among children of a given age or intellectual-maturity level, as well as what kinds of positive understanding particular children are likely to be capable of.

This chapter's discussion of young children's thinking can be summarized in a few basic points that have direct implications for teaching:

1. Children's logical thinking matures without specific teaching, but the breadth and depth of their understanding can probably be enhanced by varied, low-key experiences that offer children opportunities to practice and expand their emerging mastery of concepts such as classification, seriation, and conservation.
2. Young children can enjoy and benefit from memorizing facts and procedures, such as addition or measurement, even though they are too young to understand all of the implications of what they are doing.
3. Even simple number skills, such as counting, represent a major challenge to preschool children and should be taught slowly, with the difficulty of tasks gradually increased.
4. Young children master skills, such as arithmetic computation or measurement, in the specific forms that they have been taught and should not be assumed to generalize spontaneously to new types of problems.
5. Since young children tend to be naturally aware of the topological features of space, topology offers a useful approach for building confidence and establishing habits of thinking about spatial problems.
6. Young children need prolonged, repeated practice in mastering projective spatial relationships, particularly left and right. Distinctions such as left/right and front/back are first mastered as features of the child's own body, then as properties of other objects, and finally as relations among objects.
7. Young children often have difficulty in coordinating perspectives and predicting how things will look from viewpoints other than their own. Their skill in such tasks may improve with practice in simple situations.

8. Children who have been taught computational procedures for measuring space do not necessarily understand the general principles behind what they are doing.

Recommended Reading

Copeland, R. W. *How children learn mathematics,* 2nd edition. New York: Macmillan, 1974.

Lovell, K. *The growth of understanding in mathematics: Kindergarten through grade three*. New York: Holt, Rinehart and Winston, 1971.

Rosskopf, M. F., Steffe, L. P., & Taback, S. (Eds.). *Piagetian cognitive development research and mathematical education*. Washington, D.C.: National Council of Teachers of Mathematics, 1971.

Sauvy, H., & Sauvy, S. *The child's discovery of space*. Baltimore, Md.: Penguin Books, 1974.

Sharp, E. *Thinking is child's play*. New York: Avon Books, 1969.

CHAPTER
SIX

SUMMARY: HOW CHILDREN CHANGE AND LEARN

look at ykbir each day tread him feed him & read card.

This book is about the process of cognitive change: what children know, when they are ready to learn, and how they learn. Knowing the cognitive skills that children are likely to have can help teachers to create opportunities for children to exercise and to apply those skills.

Knowing what kinds of experiences are likely to foster the emergence of new skills can help teachers to choose classroom activities that are likely to have long-term beneficial effects on children's cognitive competence. Finally, knowing the probable *limits* of young children's capacities permits teachers to devise learning situations that stretch but do not over-burden those capacities.

A number of general conclusions about the nature of young children's minds and the ways in which teachers can help them to grow can be drawn from the book as a whole.

1. Young children naturally seek out experiences that help them expand their understanding. A teaching program adapted to children's developing cognitive abilities will capitalize on this built-in desire to learn.
2. Young children have a limited ability to control their attention, and they may need help in discovering what aspects of a situation are important. They may also profit from the teacher's efforts to reduce extraneous, distracting elements in learning situations.
3. Young children have a limited ability to recall newly learned information. Lessons for young children should be designed to present information in small doses that can be repeated until the information is securely remembered.
4. Although young children do learn by quietly watching and listening, many ideas and skills are best learned when children have opportunities for active physical and mental involvement—for touching, testing, and talking about things on their own. Such involvement enhances children's attention, memory, and ultimate understanding. One advantage of using concrete materials in the classroom is that these materials can be used to encourage children's active involvement in learning.
5. Young children's verbal fluency, communication effectiveness, and understanding of new words can be enhanced by providing opportunities for them

to practice their language skills and to observe how adults use language. Efforts to modify young children's grammar by direct teaching are, however, ill-advised. Opportunities to hear and to use language will eventually be reflected in children's grammar as well as in their other language skills.

6. Children can benefit from learning skills even though they are not yet mature enough to understand all of the logic underlying what they are doing. Young children's learning of skills such as counting is slow and is initially limited to specific situations, but practicing these elementary skills may help children as they gradually develop their understanding of the logic related to each skill.

7. Children learn what they are taught, but both the psychological and the educational literature provide ample evidence that there are no known magic activities for producing generally "intelligent" children. Children can be taught to speak well, to master mathematical computation skills, to classify, and to demonstrate understanding of mathematical logic. None of these gains, however, shows impressive generalization to other cognitive areas that have not been stressed in classroom activities (Almy, 1971; Bingham-Newman et al., 1974; Walker & Schaffarzick, 1974). The absence of generalization is undoubtedly one reason why no early-education program has been found to be consistently and generally superior to other programs (White, Day, Freeman, Hantman, & Messenger, 1973). Children's achievements in school reflect the educational priorities of their teachers (Stallings, 1975).

8. The best tests of any teaching strategy are the children's interest and their success in learning.

The application of psychological knowledge in the classroom is not likely to make the teacher's job an easy one. The evidence is consistent in indicating how very difficult it is to teach effectively. An analysis of the research literature suggests that teachers should be constantly aware of each child's current level of understanding, that every child should be given opportunities for active involvement with the learning process (with the help of an abundance of attractive materials), and that children will do unusually well only on those tasks to which considerable classroom time has been devoted. Teachers are asked to apply these findings in classrooms that are likely to be overcrowded and underequipped and to groups of children whose individual abilities and interests are likely to be tremendously varied. Yet it is the very difficulty of teaching effectively with inadequate support systems that makes it so important for teachers to learn all they can about the nature of young children and their learning processes. Our hope is that this book may increase teachers' understanding in ways that can be translated into successful classroom experiences.

REFERENCES

Abravanel, E. Choice for shape vs. textural matching by young children. *Perceptual and Motor Skills*, 1970, *31*, 527–533.

Almy, M. E. Longitudinal studies related to the classroom. In M. F. Rosskopf et al. (Eds.), *Piagetian cognitive development research and mathematical education*. Washington, D.C.: National Council of Teachers of Mathematics, 1971.

Anastasiow, N. J., & Hanes, M. L. Cognitive development and acquisition of language in three subcultural groups. *Developmental Psychology*, 1974, *10*, 703–709.

Appel, L. F., Cooper, R. G., McCarrell, N., Sims-Knight, J., Yussen, S. R., & Flavell, J. H. Development of the distinction between perceiving and memorizing. *Child Development*, 1972, *43*, 1365–1381.

Asso, D., & Wyke, M. Discrimination of spatially confusable letters by young children. *Journal of Experimental Child Psychology*, 1971, *11*, 11–20.

Baldwin, A. *Theories of child development*. New York: Wiley, 1967.

Balling, J. D., & Myers, N. A. Memory and attention in children's double alternation learning. *Journal of Experimental Child Psychology*, 1971, *11*, 448–460.

Bartlett, E. J. Selecting preschool language programs. In C. B. Cazden (Ed.), *Language in early childhood education*. Washington, D.C.: National Association for the Education of Young Children, 1972.

Berch, D. B., & Evans, R. C. Decision processes in children's recognition memory. *Journal of Experimental Child Psychology*, 1973, *16*, 148–164.

Bernstein, B. Social structure, language, and learning. *Educational Research*, 1961, *3*, 163–176.

Bingham-Newman, A. M., Saunders, R. A., & Hooper, F. H. *Logical operations instruction in the preschool*. Madison: University of Wisconsin Child and Family Studies Program, 1974.

Birch, H. G., & Belmont, L. Auditory-visual integration, intelligence, and reading ability in school children. *Perceptual and Motor Skills*, 1965, *20*, 295–305.

Blank, M. Cognitive functions of language in the preschool years. *Developmental Psychology*, 1974, *10*, 229–245.

Blank, M., & Frank, S. M. Story recall in kindergarten children: Effect of method of presentation on psycholinguistic performance. *Child Development*, 1971, *42*, 299–312.

Botvin, G. J., & Murray, F. B. The efficacy of peer modeling and social conflict in the acquisition of conservation. *Child Development*, 1975, *46*, 796–799.

Bower, T. G. R. The object in the world of the infant. *Scientific American*, April 1971, pp. 30–38.

Brainerd, C. J. Mathematical and behavioral foundations of number. *Journal of General Psychology*, 1973, *88*, 221–228. (a)

Brainerd, C. J. Order of acquisition of transitivity, conservation and class inclusion of length and weight. *Developmental Psychology,* 1973, *8,* 105–116. (b)

Brainerd, C. J., & Brainerd, S. Order of acquisition of number and quantity conservation. *Child Development,* 1972, *43,* 140.

Brown, A. L., & Campione, J. C. Color dominance in preschool children as a function of specific cue preferences. *Child Development,* 1971, *42,* 1495–1500.

Brown, A. L., & Scott, M. S. Recognition memory for pictures in preschool children. *Journal of Experimental Child Psychology,* 1971, *11,* 401–412.

Brown, R. *A first language.* Cambridge, Mass.: Harvard University Press, 1973.

Bruner, J. S., Olver, R., & Greenfield, P. M. *Studies in cognitive growth.* New York: Wiley, 1966.

Burling, R. *English in black and white.* New York: Holt, Rinehart & Winston, 1973.

Cazden, C. B. (Ed.). *Language in early childhood education.* Washington, D.C.: National Association for the Education of Young Children, 1972.

Cazden, C. B., Baratz, J. C., Labov, W., & Palmer, F. H. Language development in day care programs. In C. B. Cazden (Ed.), *Language in early childhood education.* Washington, D.C.: National Association for the Education of Young Children, 1972.

Chukovsky, K. *From two to five* (M. Morton, trans.). Berkeley: University of California Press, 1968.

Clark, E. V. On the child's acquisition of antonyms in two semantic fields. *Journal of Verbal Learning and Verbal Behavior,* 1972, *11,* 750–758.

Clark, E. V. What's in a word? In T. E. Moore (Ed.), *Cognitive development and the acquisition of language.* New York: Academic Press, 1973. (a)

Clark, E. V. Nonlinguistic strategies and the acquisition of word meanings. *Cognition,* 1973, *2,* 161–182. (b)

Clark, H. H. Space, time, semantics, and the child. In T. E. Moore (Ed.), *Cognitive development and the acquisition of language.* New York: Academic Press, 1973.

Cohen, L. B., & Salapatek, P. (Eds.). *Infant Perception: From sensation to cognition.* New York: Academic Press, 1975.

Cole, M. A developmental study of factors influencing discrimination transfer. *Journal of Experimental Child Psychology,* 1973, *16,* 126–147.

Cole, M., Gay, J., Glick, J., & Sharp, D. W. Linguistic structure and transposition. *Science,* 1969, *164,* 90–91.

Conrad, R. The chronology of the development of covert speech in children. *Developmental Psychology,* 1971, *5,* 398–405.

Cook, Nancy. Personal communication, August 1976.

Copeland, R. W. *How children learn mathematics,* 2nd edition. New York: Macmillan, 1974.

Copple, C. E., & Suci, G. J. The comparative ease of processing standard English and Black nonstandard English by lower-class Black children. *Child Development,* 1974, *45,* 1048–1053.

Corsini, D. A. Memory: Interaction of stimulus and organismic factors. *Human Development,* 1971, *14,* 227–235.

Corsini, D. A., Pick, A. D., & Flavell, J. H. Production of nonverbal mediators in young children. *Child Development,* 1968, *39,* 53–58.

Cousins, D., & Abravanel, E. Some findings relevant to the hypothesis that topological spatial features are differentiated prior to Euclidean features during growth. *British Journal of Psychology,* 1971, *62,* 475–479.

Curcio, F., Kattef, E., Levine, D., & Robbins, O. Compensation and susceptibility to conservation training. *Developmental Psychology,* 1972, *7,* 259–265.

Dahlem, N. W. Reconstitutive memory in kindergarten children revisited. *Psychonomic Science*, 1969, *17*, 101–102.

Dale, P. S. *Language development: Structure and Function.* New York: Holt, Rinehart & Winston, 1976.

DeLeon, J. L., Raslan, L. M., & Gruen, G. E. Sensory-modality effects on shape perception in preschool children. *Developmental Psychology*, 1970, *3*, 358–362.

Denney, D. R., Denney, N. W., & Zeobrowski, M. S. Alterations in the information processing strategies of young children following observation of adult models. *Developmental Psychology*, 1973, *8*, 202–208.

Denney, N. W. A developmental study of free classification in children. *Child Development*, 1972, *43*, 221–232. (a)

Denney, N. W. Free classification in preschool children. *Child Development*, 1972, *43*, 1161–1170. (b)

Dodwell, P. C. Children's understanding of number and related concepts. *Canadian Journal of Psychology*, 1960, *14*, 191–205.

Dodwell, P. C. Children's understanding of spatial concepts. *Canadian Journal of Psychology*, 1963, *17*, 141–161.

Dodwell, P. C. Children's perception and their understanding of geometrical ideas. In M. F. Rosskopf et al. (Eds.), *Piagetian cognitive development research and mathematical education.* Washington, D.C.: National Council of Teachers of Mathematics, 1971.

Donaldson, M., & Balfour, G. Less is more: A study of language comprehension in children. *British Journal of Psychology*, 1968, *59*, 461–471.

Donaldson, M., & Wales, R. On the acquisition of some relational terms. In J. R. Hayes (Ed.), *Cognition and the development of language.* New York: Wiley, 1970.

Elkind, D. Children's discovery of the conservation of mass, weight and volume: Piaget replication study II. *Journal of Genetic Psychology*, 1961, *98*, 219–227.

Elkind, D. Children's conceptions of left and right: Piaget replication study IV. *Journal of Genetic Psychology*, 1962, *99*, 267–276.

Elkind, D., & Schoenfeld, E. Identity and equivalence conservation at two age levels. *Developmental Psychology*, 1972, *6*, 529–533.

Evans, E. B. *Contemporary influences in early childhood education*, 2nd edition. New York: Holt, Rinehart & Winston, 1975.

Fajnsztejn-Pollack, G. A developmental study of decay rate in long term memory. *Journal of Experimental Child Psychology*, 1973, *16*, 225–235.

Farnham-Diggory, S. (Ed.). *Information processing in children.* New York: Academic Press, 1972.

Finkel, D. L., & Crowley, C. A. Improvement in children's long-term memory for seriated sticks: Change in memory storage or coding rules? Paper presented at the biennial meetings of the Society for Research in Child Development, Philadelphia, Pa., March 1973.

Fishbein, H. D., Lewis, S., & Kuffer, K. Children's understanding of spatial relations. *Developmental Psychology*, 1972, *7*, 21–23.

Flavell, J. H. Role-taking and communication skills in young children. In W. W. Hartup & N. L. Smothergill (Eds.), *The young child.* Washington, D.C.: National Association for the Education of Young Children, 1967.

Flavell, J. H. Developmental studies of mediated memory. In L. P. Lipsitt and H. W. Reese (Eds.), *Advances in child development and behavior*, Vol. 5. New York: Academic Press, 1970.

Flavell, J. H., Beach, D. R., & Chinsky, J. M. Spontaneous verbal rehearsal in a memory task as a function of age. *Child Development*, 1966, *37*, 283–299.

Fowler, W. Concept learning in early childhood. *Young Children*, 1965, *21*, 81–91.

Frentz, T. S. Children's comprehension of standard and negro nonstandard English sentences. *Speech Monographs*, 1971, *38*, 10–16.

Furth, H. G. Linguistic deficiency and thinking: Research with deaf subjects 1964–1969. *Psychological Bulletin*, 1971, *75*, 58–72.

Garvey, C., & Hogan, R. Social speech and social interaction: Egocentrism revisited. *Child Development*, 1973, *44*, 562–568.

Gelman, R. Conservation acquisition: A problem of learning to attend to relevant attributes. *Journal of Experimental Child Psychology*, 1969, *7*, 167–187.

Gelman, R. Logical capacity of very young children: Number invariance rules. *Child Development*, 1972, *43*, 75–90.

Genshaft, J. L., & Hirt, M. Language differences between black children and white children. *Developmental Psychology*, 1974, *10*, 451–456.

Gibson, E. J. *Principles of perceptual learning and development.* New York: Appleton-Century-Crofts, 1969.

Gibson, E. J., & Levin, H. *The psychology of reading.* Cambridge, Mass.: MIT Press, 1975.

Ginsburg, H. *The myth of the deprived child.* Englewood Cliffs, N. J.: Prentice-Hall, 1972.

Gleason, J. B. An experimental approach to improving children's communication ability. In C. B. Cazden (Ed.), *Language in early childhood education.* Washington, D.C.: National Association for the Education of Young Children, 1972.

Goodman, K. S. The reading process. In S. Smiley and J. C. Towner (Eds.), *Sixth Western symposium on learning: Language and reading.* Bellingham, Wash.: Western Washington State College, 1975.

Goodnow, J. J. Matching auditory and visual series: Modality problem or translation problem? *Child Development*, 1971, *42*, 1187–1201.

Goodnow, J. J. Social and informational aspects of cognitive and representational development. In S. Farnham-Diggory (Ed.), *Information processing in children.* New York: Academic Press, 1972.

Gruen, G. E. Experiences affecting the development of number conservation in children. *Child Development*, 1965, *36*, 963–979.

Haas, Phyllis. Personal communication, November 1974.

Hagen, J. W. Strategies for remembering. In S. Farnham-Diggory (Ed.), *Information processing in children.* New York: Academic Press, 1972.

Haith, M. M. Developmental changes in visual information processing and short-term visual memory. *Human Development*, 1971, *14*, 249–261.

Hall, J. W. Young children's memory encoding reflected in verbal discrimination learning and recognition memory performance. *Psychonomic Science*, 1971, *25*, 91–93.

Hall, J. W., & Halperin, M. S. The development of memory-encoding processes in young children. *Developmental Psychology*, 1972, *6*, 181.

Hall, W. S., & Freedle, R. O. A developmental investigation of standard and nonstandard English among Black and White children. *Human Development*, 1973, *16*, 440–464.

Harris, L. S. Discrimination of left and right and the development of the logic of relations. *Merrill-Palmer Quarterly*, 1972, *18*, 307–320.

Hartley, D. G. The effect of perceptual salience on reflective-impulsive performance differences. *Developmental Psychology*, 1976, *12*, 218–225.

Horowitz, L. M., Lampel, A. K., & Takanishi, R. N. The child's memory for unitized scenes. *Journal of Experimental Child Psychology,* 1969, *8,* 375−383.

Hoving, K. L., Coates, L., Bertucci, M., & Riccio, D. C. Reinstatement effects in children. *Developmental Psychology,* 1972, *6,* 426−429.

Hoving, K. L., Morin, R. E., & Kronick, D. C. Recognition reaction time and size of the memory set: A developmental study. *Psychonomic Science,* 1970, *21,* 247−248.

Johnson, D. L. The influences of social class and race on language test performance and spontaneous speech of preschool children. *Child Development,* 1974, *45,* 517−521.

Johnson, P. S., Warner, M., & Silleroy, R. Factors influencing children's concept identification performance with nonpreferred relevant attributes. *Journal of Experimental Child Psychology,* 1971, *11,* 430−441.

Jones, B., & Alexander, R. Developmental trends in auditory-visual cross-modal matching of spatio-temporal patterns. *Developmental Psychology,* 1974, *10,* 354−356.

Kagan, J. *Change and continuity in infancy.* New York: Wiley, 1971.

Kagan, J. Do infants think? *Scientific American,* 1972, *226,* 774.

Katz, J. M. Reflection-impulsivity and color-form sorting. *Child Development,* 1971, *42,* 745−754.

Kersh, Mildred E. Personal communication, December 1974.

Kingsley, P. R., & Hagen, J. W. Induced vs. spontaneous rehearsal in STM in nursery school children. *Developmental Psychology,* 1969, *1,* 40−46.

Kratochwill, T. R., & Goldman, J. A. Developmental changes in children's judgments of age. *Developmental Psychology,* 1973, *9,* 358−362.

Krauss, R. M., & Glucksberg, S. Socialization of communication skills. In R. A. Hoppe, G. A. Milton, & E. C. Simmel (Eds.), *Early experiences and the processes of socialization.* New York: Academic Press, 1970.

Kuhlman, E. S., & Wolking, W. D. Development of within- and cross-modal matching ability in the auditory and visual sense modalities. *Developmental Psychology,* 1972, *7,* 365.

Labov, W. Some sources of reading problems for Negro speakers of nonstandard English. In J. C. Baratz & R. W. Shuy (Eds.), *Teaching Black children to read.* Washington, D.C.: Center for Applied Linguistics, 1969.

Labov, W. *The study of nonstandard English.* Champaign, Ill.: National Council of Teachers of English, 1970.

Labov, W. *Language in the inner city.* Philadelphia: University of Pennsylvania Press, 1972.

LaCivita, A., Kean, J. M., & Yamamoto, M. Socioeconomic status of children and the acquisition of grammar. *Journal of Educational Research,* 1966, *60,* 71−74.

Langacker, R. W. *Language and its structure.* New York: Harcourt Brace Jovanovich, 1973.

Larsen, G. V., & Flavell, J. H. Verbal factors in compensation performance and the relation between conservation and compensation. *Child Development,* 1970, *41,* 965−978.

Laurendeau, M., & Pinard, A. *The development of the concept of space in the child.* New York: International Universities Press, 1970.

Lehman, E. B. Selective strategies in children's attention to task-relevant information. *Child Development,* 1972, *43,* 197−209.

Lloyd, B. B. Studies of conservation with Yoruba children of differing ages and experience. *Child Development,* 1971, *42,* 415−428.

Locke, J. L., & Fehr, F. S. Young children's use of the speech code in a recall task. *Journal of Experimental Child Psychology*, 1970, *10*, 367–373.

Looft, W. R. Children's judgments of age. *Child Development*, 1971, *42*, 1282–1284.

Lovell, K. The development of some mathematical ideas in elementary school pupils. In N. F. Rosskopf et al. (Eds.), *Piagetian cognitive development research and mathematical education*. Washington, D.C.: National Council of Teachers of Mathematics, 1971. (a)

Lovell, K. *The growth of understanding in mathematics: Kindergarten through grade three*. New York: Holt, Rinehart & Winston, 1971. (b)

Lovell, K. Some studies involving spatial ideas. In M. F. Rosskopf et al. (Eds.), *Piagetian cognitive development research and mathematical education*. Washington, D.C.: National Council of Teachers of Mathematics, 1971. (c)

Maccoby, E. E., & Konrad, K. W. The effect of preparatory set on selective listening: Developmental trends. *Monographs of the Society for Research in Child Development*, 1967, *32* (No. 4).

Maratsos, M. P. Decrease in the understanding of the word "big" in preschool children. *Child Development*, 1973, *44*, 747–752. (a)

Maratsos, M. P. Nonegocentric communication abilities in preschool children. *Child Development*, 1973, *44*, 697–700. (b)

Maratsos, M. P. When is a high thing the big one? *Developmental Psychology*, 1974, *10*, 367–375.

McCarson, C. S., & Daves, W. R. Development of free recall of object names as a function of overt verbalization and intracategory variation. *Developmental Psychology*, 1972, *6*, 178.

McGurk, H. The salience of orientation in young children's perception of form. *Child Development*, 1972, *43*, 1047–1052.

McNeill, D. Developmental psycholinguistics. In F. Smith & G. A. Miller (Eds.), *The genesis of language*. Cambridge, Mass.: MIT Press, 1966.

Meichenbaum, D. H. The nature and modification of impulsive children: Training children to talk to themselves. Research Report No. 23, Department of Psychology, University of Waterloo, Waterloo, Ont., 1971.

Meichenbaum, D. H., & Goodman, J. Training impulsive children to talk to themselves: A means of developing self control. *Journal of Abnormal Psychology*, 1971, *77*, 115–126.

Millar, S. *The psychology of play*. London: Penguin, 1968.

Millar, S. Visual and haptic cue utilization by preschool children: The recognition of visual and haptic stimuli presented separately and together. *Journal of Experimental Child Psychology*, 1971, *12*, 88–94.

Millar, S. Effects of instructions to visualize stimuli during delay on visual recognition by preschool children. *Child Development*, 1972, *43*, 1073–1075.

Miller, G. A. The magical number seven, plus or minus two: Some limits on our capacity for processing information. *Psychological Review*, 1956, *63*, 81–97.

Miller, R. M., & LeBlanc, J. M. Experimental analysis of the effect of detailed and minimal instructions upon the acquisition of pre-academic skills. Paper presented at the 81st Annual Convention of the American Psychological Association, Montreal, Canada, August 27–31, 1973.

Moynahan, E., & Glick, J. Relation between identity conservation and equivalence conservation within four conceptual domains. *Developmental Psychology*, 1972, *6*, 247–251.

Muehl, S., & Kremenak, S. Ability to match information within and between auditory and visual sense modalities and subsequent reading achievement. *Journal of Educational Psychology*, 1966, *57*, 230−238.

Mueller, E. The maintenance of verbal exchanges between young children. *Child Development*, 1972, *43*, 930−938.

Murray, F. B. Acquisition of conservation through social interaction. *Developmental Psychology*, 1972, *6*, 1−6.

Nodine, C. F., & Lang, N. S. Development of visual scanning strategies for differentiating words. *Developmental Psychology*, 1971, *5*, 221−232.

O'Bryan, K. G., & Boersma, F. S. Eye movements, perceptual activity, and conservation development. *Journal of Experimental Child Psychology*, 1971, *12*, 157−169.

Odom, R. D., Astor, E. C., & Cunningham, J. G. Effects of perceptual salience on the matrix task performance of four- and six-year-old children. *Child Development*, 1975, *46*, 758−762.

Odom, R. D., & Guzman, R. D. Development of hierarchies of dimensional salience. *Developmental Psychology*, 1972, *6*, 271−287.

Osborn, J. Teaching a teaching language to disadvantaged children. In M. A. Brottman (Ed.), *Language remediation for the disadvantaged preschool child*. Monographs of the Society for Research in Child Development, 1968, *33*, 36−48 (No. 124).

Papalia, D. E., & Hooper, F. M. A developmental comparison of identity and equivalence conservations. *Journal of Experimental Child Psychology*, 1971, *12*, 347−361.

Perlmutter, M., & Myers, N. A. Recognition memory development in two- to four-year-olds. *Developmental Psychology*, 1974, *10*, 447−450.

Peters, D. L. Verbal mediators and cue discrimination in the transition from nonconservation of number. *Child Development*, 1970, *41*, 707−721.

Peterson, C. L., Danner, F. W., & Flavell, J. H. Developmental changes in children's response to three indications of communicative failure. *Child Development*, 1972, *43*, 1463−1468.

Piaget, J. *Play, dreams, and imitation in childhood*. New York: Norton, 1951.

Piaget, J. *The origins of intelligence in children*. New York: International Universities Press, 1952 (Norton Library Edition, 1963).

Piaget, J. *The language and thought of the child*, 3rd edition. London: Routledge, 1959.

Piaget, J. *On the development of memory and identity* (E. Duckworth, trans.). Worcester, Mass.: Clark University Press, 1968.

Piaget, J. *Science of education and the psychology of the child*. New York: Viking Press, 1971. Translation copyright 1970 by Grossman Publishers.

Piaget, J., & Inhelder, B. *The child's conception of space*. London: Routledge and Kegan Paul, 1956.

Pick, A. D., Frankel, D. G., & Hess, V. L. Children's attention: The development of selectivity. In E. M. Hetherington (Ed.), *Review of child development research*, Vol. 5. Chicago: University of Chicago Press, 1975.

Pick, H. L., & Pick, A. D. Sensory and perceptual development. In P. H. Mussen (Ed.), *Carmichael's manual of child psychology*. New York: Wiley, 1970. Pp. 773−848.

Potter, M. C. On perceptual recognition. In J. S. Bruner et al. (Eds.), *Studies in cognitive growth*. New York: Wiley, 1966.

Pufall, P. B., & Shaw, R. E. Precocious thoughts on number: The long and short of it. *Developmental Psychology*, 1972, *7*, 62−69.

Read, C. Preschool children's knowledge of English phonology. *Harvard Educational Review*, 1971, *41*, 1−34.

Reese, H. W. Models of memory and models of development. *Human Development,* 1973, *16,* 397−416.

Reese, H. W., & Lipsitt, L. P. *Experimental child psychology.* New York: Academic Press, 1970.

Reilly, D. H. Auditory-visual integration, school demographic features and reading achievement. *Perceptual and Motor Skills,* 1972, *35,* 995−1001.

Resnick, L. B., Wang, M. C., & Kaplan, J. Behavior analysis in curriculum design: A hierarchically sequenced introductory mathematics curriculum. University of Pittsburgh Learning Research and Development Center, Monograph 2, 1970.

Resnick, L. B., Wang, M. C., & Kaplan, J. Task analysis in curriculum design: A hierarchically sequenced introductory mathematics curriculum. *Journal of Applied Behavior Analysis,* 1973, *6,* 382−401.

Robinson, J. P., & London, P. Labeling and imaging as aids to memory. *Child Development,* 1971, *42,* 641−644.

Roodin, M. L., & Gruen, G. E. The role of memory in making transitive judgments. *Journal of Experimental Child Psychology,* 1970, *10,* 264−275.

Rosenthal, T. L., & Zimmerman, B. S. Modeling by exemplification and instruction in training conservation. *Developmental Psychology,* 1972, *6,* 382−401.

Ross, B. M., & Youniss, J. Ordering of nonverbal items in children's recognition memory. *Journal of Experimental Child Psychology,* 1969, *8,* 20−32.

Rossi, S., & Wittrock, N. C. Developmental shifts in verbal recall between mental ages two and three. *Child Development,* 1971, *42,* 333−338.

Rosskopf, M. F., Steffe, L. P., & Taback, S. (Eds.). *Piagetian cognitive development research and mathematical education.* Washington, D.C.: National Council of Teachers of Mathematics, 1971.

Ryan, S. M., Hegion, A. G., & Flavell, J. H. Nonverbal mnemonic mediation in preschool children. *Child Development,* 1970, *41,* 539−549.

Salatas, H., & Flavell, J. H. Behavioral and metamnemonic indicators of strategic behaviors under remember instructions in first grade. *Child Development,* 1976, *47,* 81−89.

Sauvy, H., & Sauvy, S. *The child's discovery of space.* Baltimore, Md.: Penguin Books, 1974.

Schell, D. J. Conceptual behavior in young children: Learning to shift dimensional attention. *Journal of Experimental Child Psychology,* 1971, *12,* 72−87.

Selman, R. L. Taking another's perspective: Role-taking development in early childhood. *Child Development,* 1971, *42,* 1721−1734.

Shantz, C. U., & Watson, J. S. Spatial abilities and spatial egocentrism in the young child. *Child Development,* 1971, *42,* 171−181.

Sharp, E. *Thinking is child's play.* New York: Avon Books, 1969.

Sheingold, K. Developmental differences in intake and storage ot visual information. *Journal of Experimental Child Psychology,* 1973, *16,* 1−11.

Shriner, T. H., & Miner, L. Morphological structures in the language of disadvantaged and advantaged children. *Journal of Speech and Hearing Research,* 1968, *11,* 605−610.

Siegler, R. S., & Liebert, R. M. Effects of presenting relevant rules and complete feedback on the conservation of liquid quantity task. *Developmental Psychology,* 1972, *7,* 133−138.

Sigel, I. E. The development of classificatory skills in young children: A training program. In W. W. Hartup (Ed.), *The young child* (Vol. 2). Washington, D.C.: National Association for the Education of Young Children, 1972.

Sinclair, H. Number and measurement. In M. F. Rosskopf et al. (Eds.), *Piagetian cognitive developmental research and mathematical education*. Washington, D.C.: National Council of Teachers of Mathematics, 1970.

Sinclair-de Zwart, H. Language acquisition and cognitive development. In T. E. Moore (Ed.), *Cognitive development and the acquisition of language*. New York: Academic Press, 1973.

Smith, F. The role of prediction in reading. In S. Smiley & J. C. Towner (Eds.), *Sixth Western symposium on learning: Language and reading*. Bellingham, Wash.: Western Washington State College, 1975.

Smothergill, N. L., Olson, F., & Moore, S. G. The effects of manipulation of teacher communication style in the preschool. *Child Development*, 1971, *42*, 1227–1239.

Spence, C. M. Relational concepts in the language and thought of deaf and hearing preschool children. Unpublished doctoral dissertation, University of Washington, 1973.

Spence, J. T. The distracting effects of material reinforcers in the discrimination learning of lower- and middle-class children. *Child Development*, 1970, *41*, 103–112.

Stallings, J. Implementation and child effects of teaching practices in Follow Through classrooms. *Monographs of the Society for Research in Child Development*, 1975, *40*, (Nos. 7–8, Serial No. 163).

Stodolsky, S., & Lesser, G. Learning patterns in the disadvantaged. *Harvard Educational Review*, 1967, *37*, 546–593.

Strayer, J., & Ames, E. W. Stimulus orientation and the apparent developmental lag between perception and performance. *Child Development*, 1972, *43*, 1345–1354.

Thomson, C. *Skills for young children*. Lawrence, Kans.: Department of Human Development, University of Kansas, 1972.

Thurm, A. T., & Glanzer, M. Free recall in children: Long-term store vs. short-term store. *Psychonomic Science*, 1971, *23*, 175–176.

Trabasso, T. Memory and inference. Colloquium presented at the University of Washington, Seattle, February 13, 1973.

Turnure, J. E. Control of orienting behavior in children under five years of age. *Developmental Psychology*, 1971, *4*, 16–24.

Vygotsky, L. S. *Thought and speech*. Cambridge, Mass.: MIT Press, 1962.

Walker, D. F., & Schaffarzick, J. Comparing curricula. *Review of Educational Research*, 1974, *44*, 83–111.

Wang, M. C., Resnick, L. B., & Boozer, R. F. The sequence of development of some early mathematics behaviors. *Child Development*, 1971, *42*, 1767–1778.

Weikart, D. P., McClelland, D., Hiatt, L., Mainwaring, S., & Weathers, T. *The language training curriculum*. Ypsilanti, Mich.: High/Scope Educational Research Foundation, 1970.

Weikart, D. P., McClelland, D., Smith, S. A., Kluge, J., Hudson, A., & Taylor, C. *The cognitive curriculum*. Ypsilanti, Mich.: High/Scope Educational Research Foundation, 1970.

Weikart, D. P., Rogers, L., Adcock, C., & McClelland, D. *The cognitively oriented curriculum*. Washington, D.C.: National Association for the Education of Young Children, 1971.

White, K. M. Conceptual style and conceptual ability in kindergarten through eighth grade. *Child Development*, 1971, *42*, 1652–1656.

White, S. H., Day, M. C., Freeman, P. K., Hantman, S. A., & Messenger, K. P. *Federal programs for young children: Review and recommendations*. Washington, D.C.: U.S. Government Printing Office, 1973 (NTIS No. OS-74-100).

Williams, K. G., & Goulet, L. R. The effects of cueing and constraint conditions on children's free recall performance. *Journal of Experimental Child Psychology,* 1975, *19,* 464–475.

Winer, G. Induced set and acquisition of number conservation. *Child Development,* 1968, *39,* 195–205.

Wohlwill, J. F. A study of the development of the number concept by scalogram analysis. *Journal of Genetic Psychology,* 1960, *97,* 345–377.

Wohlwill, J. F., & Lowe, R. C. Experimental analysis of the development of the conservation of number. *Child Development,* 1972, *33,* 153–167.

Wolff, P. The role of stimulus-correlated activity in children's recognition of non-sense forms. *Journal of Experimental Child Psychology,* 1972, *14,* 427–441.

Wolff, P., Levin, S. R., & Longobardi, E. T. Motoric mediation in children's paired associate learning: Effects of visual and tactual contact. *Journal of Experimental Child Psychology,* 1972, *74,* 176–183.

Yussen, S. R. Determinants of visual attention and recall in observational learning by preschoolers & second graders. *Developmental Psychology,* 1974, *10,* 93–100.

Yussen, S. R. Some reflections on strategic remembering in young children. Paper presented at the biennial meetings of the Society for Research in Child Development, Denver, April 1975.

Zaporozhets, A. V. The development of perception in the preschool child. In P. H. Mussen (Ed.), *European research in child development.* Monographs of the Society for Research in Child Development, 1965, *30* (Serial No. 100), 82–101.

INDEX